# CHOCOLATE

# CHOCOLATE

deliciously indulgent recipes for chocolate lovers

RYLAND
PETERS
& SMALL

LONDON NEW YORK

## Maxine Clark

photography by Peter Cassidy

**Dedication**
To Steve, a truly dedicated taster, tester and
gifted stylist

**Design, photographic art direction
and prop styling** Steve Painter
**Editor** Céline Hughes
**Production Manager** Patricia Harrington
**Publishing Director** Alison Starling

**Food Stylist** Maxine Clark
**Assistant Food Stylists** Joanna Lee, Jacks Clarke

**Indexer** Diana Le Core

**Author's acknowledgements**
Grateful thanks are due to the following people
for help and advice:

Chloé Doutre-Roussel
The Chocolate Society
Martin Christy (www.seventypercent.com)
Pia Scavia, my Italian secret agent
Giacomo Biodi, Laboratorio Artigianale Giraudi
(www.giraudi.it)
Lourdes Delgado, Ecuador
Graciela and Ian Mursell of Mexicolore, London
Dr. C.J. Turnbull, International Cocoa Germplasm
Database, University of Reading
Dr Andrew Daymond, Cocoa Quarantine Project,
University of Reading
Simon Harris of Barry Callebaut, UK

Ryland Peters & Small
Céline, my editor, for keeping me firmly on track
Alison Starling, for suggesting the book

The photographic team
Pete, you made it look so wonderful in both good
and bad lights and a tight schedule
Steve, a designer with hidden styling talents –
thanks for a beautiful, sensitive job
Jo, you are a joy to have in the kitchen!

First published in the United Kingdom in 2007
by Ryland Peters & Small
20–21 Jockey's Fields
London WC1R 4BW
www.rylandpeters.com

10 9 8 7 6 5 4 3 2 1

Text © Maxine Clark 2007
Design and photographs
© Ryland Peters & Small 2007

ISBN 978 1 84597 462 6

A catalogue record for this book
is available from the British Library.

Printed and bound in China

**Notes**
• All spoon measurements are level unless
otherwise stated.
• Uncooked or partially cooked eggs should not
be served to the very old, frail, young children,
pregnant women or those with compromised
immune systems.

# CONTENTS

# CHOCOLATE IS GOOD FOR YOU

If chocolate was considered the food of the gods by the ancient Aztec and Mayan civilizations, who are we to argue? We have always known that eating it makes us feel good (if a little guilty), but modern scientific research by The International Cocoa Organization (ICCO) has shown that the finely ground bean of the *Theobroma cacao* tree can be beneficial to health, and more than that – to personal well-being. In this sense, it's a bit of a wonder food.

We're not talking about chocolate in the form of sugary, mass-produced candy bars. Proper chocolate made with over 60% cocoa solids and few additives other than a little sugar and vanilla, when consumed in small doses, *is* good for you.

For chocoholics, eating chocolate is an incredible sensory experience: firstly, its rich and volatile aroma is released when the wrapping is reverently removed or the lid tentatively lifted from the box. Next comes the sight of its dark, mysterious and lustrous form, then the sharp, satisfying snap as it breaks or is bitten. Finally, the longed-for moment when the chocolate is placed on the tongue and left to melt, gradually producing an explosion of hedonistic flavours (tropical fruit, liquorice, tobacco, nuts) trapped within the crushed cacao bean and awaiting their release triggered by body heat.

This inimitable process is what gives chocolate its fabled aphrodisiac qualities, since there is in fact no proven scientific evidence for its aphrodisiac status. However, it *can* trigger the release of serotonin and endorphins, both of which contribute to that 'feel-good factor'. It also contains phenylethylamine, an amine known to effect aphrodisiac symptoms (and good for relieving hangovers!) A companion of the Spanish conquistador H. Cortès, who was offered cocoa on landing in Mexico in 1519, is recorded to have said: "... the pleasure of consuming chocolate keeps one travelling all day. It keeps exhaustion away, without one feeling the need to eat or to drink."

However, there *are* several scientific facts to show that chocolate is good for you. A 100-g bar of dark chocolate (60–70% cocoa solids – see page 15 for an explanation of cocoa solids) is packed with naturally occurring minerals, giving the following RDA (Recommended Daily Allowance): magnesium 33%, phosphorous 30%, potassium 27%, copper 25%, iron 20% and calcium 13%. Dark chocolate is one of the foods richest in antioxidants, which have been shown to protect against the damaging effects of free radicals in the body. In fact, it is second only (I am reliably informed) to the prune – so you can imagine how good for you the Polish speciality of a prune dipped in dark chocolate is!

It's also good to know that cocoa butter contains 'good' fats similar to those found in olive oil. A 100-g bar made from 72% cocoa solids contains 41 g fat – but 34 g of this is unsaturated fat, which raises good cholesterol (HDL), protects the heart and lowers bad cholesterol (LDL). That leaves only 7 g saturated fat, the harmful effects of which are counterbalanced by the unsaturated fats. Thanks to modern scientific research, cacao flavonoids have been found to have a stronger antioxidant effect than those found in red wine or green tea. Cacao flavonoids can help to reduce the risk of heart attack (and possibly cancer), protect against arthritis and even act as a natural antihistamine. Wow – we always knew chocolate was good for us, but we never imagined it was this good!

Theobromine, the alkaloid contained in cacao beans, resembles caffeine in its action, but its effect on the central nervous system is much less powerful, so it can't really be seen as a stimulant. In order to discern any effects, you would have to eat masses, and as we know, too much of anything is bad for you. We must take all this scientific evidence (often cited by chocolate producers) with a pinch of salt and never rely on chocolate alone to replace a healthy balanced diet – view it as a dietary supplement to be taken in moderation and regularly.

Now to dispel a couple of nagging chocolate myths, so that we can appreciate it as a life-enhancing part of our diet. Eating chocolate does not cause acne. The UK Food Standards Agency, the American Dietetic Association and the American Academy of Dermatology are adamant that there is no link between chocolate and acne. It's all about balance – over-dosing on any food causes imbalance and dietary problems.

Cocoa and chocolate alone do not damage your teeth – what's harmful is usually the high quantity of sugar in poor-quality, mass-produced chocolate bars. In fact, cacao naturally contains fluoride that fights plaque and oral bacteria. Scientific research and pure common sense show us that the fruit of the cacao tree itself isn't harmful to health – it is the addition of too much sugar and vegetable fat to make low-grade chocolate that makes it addictive and heart-stopping.

Purists and chocolate lovers who would like to make the most of chocolate as a health food should try eating raw cacao nibs and cacao pulp. These are both seen to be health-giving natural foods, rich in antioxidants. Cacao nibs can even be used in baking instead of chocolate chips. However, be aware they *will* taste bitter as they are pure cacao bean, so be sure to use them in a recipe containing sugar.

All those who love chocolate know in their hearts that the purer the chocolate, the better it is for you. I recommend a daily prescription of one small square of best-quality dark chocolate, savoured slowly first thing in the morning (when the palate is at its freshest), to give yourself a palpable lift, as well as the best possible start to the day. Failing that, keep the whole household happy with my chocolate cakes and teabreads, that just get better for maturing for a day or two in the cake tin. Make a grumpy child happy by baking a batch of Chocolate Brownies or some Chocolate Chip Cookies with them after school. Surprise a down-in-the-dumps friend with a box of homemade Truffles – best shared with a glass of deep, rich red wine or port to help the digestion. Delight dinner guests with dark and mysterious Chocolate Cardamom Truffle Cake or little pots of darkest Chocolate Mousse. Drop round and treat your Mum to a lighter-than-air Chocolate Madeleine over a cup of coffee. There's a recipe for every mood and moment in this book – try one today and you'll feel all the better for it. Chocolate is THE best first aid!

# SOUTH AMERICAN ORIGINS AND CHOCOLATE COMES TO EUROPE

Based on pictorial evidence in carvings, paintings and medieval manuscripts, we know that that the cacao bean was grown and used in tropical pre-Columbian Mesoamerica (Central America) by the Olmecs, Maya, Toltecs and Aztecs (from whom we get the original name of chocolate – *cacauatl* or *xocolatl*). This takes legendary cocoa as far back as 2000 B.C.

The peoples of Mesoamerica instinctively knew how to get the best out of unpalatable cacao beans to turn them into something appealing. They dried them in the sun, then roasted them and finally ground them on the traditional three-legged *metate* (grinding stone), heated from beneath by glowing coals. There are paintings of Mayan women kneeling over these sloping *metate* (see picture, right), punishingly grinding away with the rolling pin-like *mano* to produce the butter-wet cocoa liquor used to make their foaming drink, *cacauatl*.

The expansionist Aztecs adopted the cultivation of cacao from the Maya in the fourteenth century and prepared a similar drink, *xocolatl*, where cacao beans were roasted, ground and mixed with boiling water, chilli and spices to produce a foamy liquid. These drinks, often thickened with maize meal, were considered nourishing, providing essential fats and antioxidants. The best beans were even used as offerings in sacred ceremonies – representing life-blood itself. Both Maya and Aztecs used cacao beans as currency in trading (originally mistaken by Columbus on his first encounter for worthless nuts) and as tribute money and taxes collected from conquered peoples. It was the conspicuous consumption of chocolate by the Aztec elite before the masses that furthered its prestige.

The history of chocolate in Europe begins with the Spanish conquest of Mexico in the sixteenth century and the trade between the two lands. The Spaniards had recognized only the medicinal and health benefits attached to cocoa by the native peoples and took this custom of drinking chocolate back with them to the Spanish court.

The taste for chocolate gradually spread throughout the elite households of Europe. It was made more palatable to European tastes by flavouring it with vanilla, cinnamon, aniseed, chilli and black pepper, colouring it red with *acciote* and sweetening it with newly discovered cane sugar. And it was now being served hot, not cold. The foam on top of chocolate was much prized and was produced using a hand-held rotary whisk or *molinillo*. Only the wealthy could afford to drink chocolate, as both cocoa and sugar were expensive imports. Baroque Europe deemed it healthful and it became so fashionable that a vessel called a *mancerina* was invented so that it could be drunk at court without spilling and thus ruining a gown. The French had oblique-handled pots, *chocolatières*, with an integrated wooden *moussoir* and beakers with saucers to catch the drips.

Eventually, Spain and many other mainland European nations established colonial plantations for growing cacao and sugar. For centuries, chocolate remained a handmade luxury. The Spanish learned from the Aztecs how to make a solid, portable and storable chocolate that could make an instant drink, and this practice of making cakes, balls or bricks spread rapidly throughout Europe and as far as Samoa, establishing itself as the forerunner of our modern-day chocolate bar.

Chocolate reached Britain in the seventeenth century via Jamaican cacao plantations 'liberated' in 1655 by Oliver Cromwell from the Spanish. The drink infiltrated the coffee shops, and anyone who could afford it could drink it – in Britain chocolate had lost the courtly elitism of continental Europe. The English adopted the custom of adding sherry sack, milk and egg yolks to enrich the drink, and drank it out of shallow bowls. It was through the British colonization of America that chocolate became known again as a drink.

The first European chocolate factory appeared in Bayonne, Southwest France, in 1761. Then, with the invention in 1778 of the first hydraulic machine for crushing and mixing the chocolate paste, followed in 1819 by the first steam-powered production plant, mass production made solid chocolate affordable to a much broader public. In the nineteenth century, the importance of drinking chocolate declined and solid eating chocolate started to grow in importance and with it the birth of some of the great chocolate dynasties we know today.

*Top left: a Samoan chocolate and spice ball, whole and grated*

# THE CHOCOLATE PROCESS
## HOW IT GETS FROM TREE TO BAR

You only have to taste a raw, bland cacao bean to realize what a truly ingenious process it is to turn it into the aromatic chocolate we know today. Tasting a dried cacao bean or a cacao nib will make you wonder what the Spaniards ever saw in the bitter, unpleasant bean in the first place. The chocolate-making process is nothing short of miraculous – pure alchemy!

### A FEW CHOCOLATE TERMS EXPLAINED

**Cacao tree** The tropical tree that produces cacao beans. It was officially classified in 1753 by Swedish scientist Carl von Linnaeus. He deemed cacao so important that he named the tree *Theobroma cacao*. The name derives from the ancient Greek 'theos' meaning 'god' and 'broma' meaning 'food'. This was added as a prefix to the original native name of 'cacao'.

**Cacao pod** The fruit of the cacao tree – a leathery oval pod which contains cacao beans and pulp. It is sometimes known as a *cabosse*.

**Cacao bean** The seed of the cacao tree, which is only called a cacao bean once it is removed from the pod.

**Cacao nib** The meat of the cacao bean after the shell is removed in the chocolate production process. Cacao nibs sold in health food shops are usually cracked or chopped.

**Cocoa liquor** Also called cocoa mass, the oily chocolate paste produced by grinding the cacao nibs. It is the basic ingredient in all chocolate products. (It does *not* contain any alcohol.)

**Conching** Cocoa liquor, cocoa butter and sugar are blended and placed in large agitators called 'conches' that stir and grind the mixture under heat.

**Dutch processing or Dutching** A method invented by Dutchman C. J. van Houten of treating the cacao nib or cocoa liquor with an alkali solution after roasting. This reduces the acidity in the bean by increasing the pH level from about 5.0 to 8.0.

Let's start by looking at the cacao tree itself. Being tropical, it loves humidity and it will only grow in a thin belt around the equator within the latitudes of 20° South and 20° North. It also needs the shelter of other trees growing around it. Bizarrely,

*Left: cacao pods in all their vivid colours*

cacao pods grow directly from the trunk of the tree and the larger branches (known as 'cauliflory'). The tree is in bloom almost all year round and annually produces around 50,000 flowers. The beautiful, delicate, spidery flowers have no scent and are difficult to pollinate – they are pollinated by a type of midge that only lives under the canopy of the taller trees protecting the cacao trees. The tree matures for 10 years before producing quality fruit and can grow to about 8 m. Each tree may produce up to 50 pods a year, only giving about 7–9 kg beans in total.

Ripe cacao pods are very colourful, ranging from yellow, through orange to red and purple. The pods take about four to eight months to ripen on the tree before harvesting, depending on the variety. Each pod contains about 30 oval-shaped cacao beans surrounded by a slightly sour-sweet fruity pulp. This pulp is delicious and very nutritious in its own right. At this stage if you taste a fresh bean and the pulp, there is absolutely no hint of chocolate! Each cacao bean consists of about 5% water, 54% cocoa butter, 11.5% protein, 9% starch and many other elements including aromatic oils and small amounts of the stimulants theobromine and caffeine.

### BEAN TYPES

There are three types of cacao beans: Criollo, Forastero and Trinitario.

**Criollo** are the rarest and most expensive of all cacao beans and are therefore 'The King'. The name means 'native' in Spanish, and was originally discovered by Christopher Columbus in 1502 on the island of Guanaja, Honduras. It is found growing in the rich soil and mild climate of South and Central America. It has a low yield and an extremely fine aroma and low acidity. Nowadays it is often cross-bred with Trinitario for better yields and accounts for 1–4% of the world's production.

**Forastero** means 'foreigner' in Spanish, as the beans were introduced to European-owned plantations in the early twentieth century. They are the most commonly grown cacao bean, are grown mainly in West Africa and the Amazonian Highlands, and make up about 80–90% of the world's production. Although the trees are vigorous and high yielding, the beans lack aroma and tend to be bitter. However, there are always exceptions, and a name often mentioned by professionals in the chocolate industry is Arriba (or Cacao Nacional) from Ecuador. This is a sought after Forastero bean with a flowery, fruity fragrance which cannot be grown outside Ecuador.

**Trinitario** beans are believed to be a hybrid of Criollo and Forastero, emerging after disease destroyed most of the native Criollo trees on Trinidad. 30 years later, the Forastero variety was imported and planted on the island. The few remaining Criollo trees began to hybridize with these new trees producing the new variety of Trinitario. The trees are robust and high yielding, with good, aromatic beans. They are grown mainly in Indonesia, Sri Lanka, South America and the Caribbean Islands. About 10–15% of the world's cocoa production is Trinitario.

FROM PODS TO CHOCOLATE BAR

Although the cacao tree continuously produces flowers and fruit, the main harvesting seasons are November to January and May to July. The harvesting is done very carefully by hand, using machetes, so as not to damage the trunk. Being very susceptible to disease, any damage to the tree would weaken it. Once the pods are harvested, each one is opened by hand and the beans with their surrounding soft pulp are removed. The whole lot is layered in pierced fermentation boxes or baskets between banana leaves. The pulp liquefies and drains out of the bottom of the box and the beans ferment. This generally takes three to seven days. Proper fermentation is the key to developing a full and rounded aroma, and less scrupulous farmers often cut the process out.

**Drying** The beans must be dried to prolong the shelf life when stored. Their water content is reduced from 60% to about 7% before the beans can be graded and stored. Beans are generally slowly sun-dried or dried in special rooms like giant airing cupboards. The longer the drying process, the better the flavour in the bean. Again, unscrupulous processors speed-dry them over wood fires giving the beans an undesirable smoky flavour that will not disappear. Dried beans are known as 'almendras' – the Spanish word for almonds.

**Roasting** It is careful roasting that really brings out the colour and what we all recognize as true chocolate flavour in the bean. Different bean types require different roasting times. Bean types are roasted separately then mixed together when creating a blend.

**Winnowing** After roasting, the cacao bean shells are removed leaving brittle cacao nibs. The shells are sold for use in medicine and as mulch for gardens.

**Grinding** The nibs are ground to an oily paste resembling dark brown peanut butter. This is called cocoa liquor (or mass) and only now begins to smell of chocolate. Then, either the cocoa liquor is further pressed, through a process called Dutching, into cocoa butter and cocoa (usually only done with low-quality beans for the mass market) or the liquor is ground again to produce a finer paste to be made into chocolate – both cheap chocolate and expensive chocolate. The cocoa butter is often deodorized to make it more useful to other industries, such as the beauty industry. Good white chocolate is made with non-deodorized cocoa butter.

**Conching** After the grinding, a process called conching takes place. Other ingredients, such as sugar, extra cocoa butter, powdered milk (for milk chocolate), vanilla and sometimes the stabilizer lecithin are mixed in, then the cocoa liquor is stirred and mixed at a temperature of about 82°C (180°F) for between four and 70 hours – less time is required for inferior chocolate. The friction between the sugar crystals and the cacao particles causes further polishing and refining and a chemical change takes place in the mix, giving the chocolate its fullest mellow, ripe and round flavour and silken smooth texture. The liquid chocolate is then stored in warm tanks until ready for the next stage.

**Tempering** The chocolate temperature is raised then lowered so that the crystals of cocoa butter re-align and will make the chocolate shiny and crisp when set. Once tempered, the chocolate is poured into moulds, which are tapped or shaken to expel any air bubbles trapped in the chocolate, then the moulds are cooled, the chocolate tipped out and wrapped. After this, correct storage is all-important or the chocolate could be ruined. Thus the bean finally makes it to the bar – what a magnificent journey it undergoes to become the world's most popular and sublimely harmless fix!

*Right: cacao beans*

# CHOCOLATE TYPES

In essence, there are three familiar types of chocolate, loosely described as dark, milk and white. However, there has been a revolution in chocolate-making, transforming it into something akin to wine- or olive oil-making. We are now seeing single-bean chocolate, single-estate chocolate, organic chocolate, Fairtrade chocolate, chocolate made in the antique style, with a gritty texture from roughly crushed beans and coarse sugar and flavoured with cinnamon or chilli, to pure chocolate and spice balls made to be grated into savoury dishes or hot drinks. The list is endless, but here are some basic chocolate descriptions to help the home cook.

**Dark chocolate** contains no powdered milk and has a minimum of 43% cocoa solids (35% in the USA).

**Milk chocolate** has a minimum of 25% cocoa solids (10% in the USA), is enriched with powdered milk for a creamy, luxurious texture and has more added sugar.

**White chocolate** has no cocoa liquor, and is therefore not considered real chocolate, but rather confectionery. It is made from a combination of cocoa butter, sugar, milk solids and usually flavoured with vanilla. The worst is adulterated with other vegetable fats, is flavoured with synthetic vanillin and is very white in colour. The best are ivory-coloured, have a high cocoa butter percentage, milk solids for creamy richness and are flavoured with real vanilla and may contain lecithin. In the USA it must be called 'white confectionery coating'. It has a short shelf-life, is a little tricky to work with and can pick up alien flavours.

**Chocolate-flavoured cake covering** is full of vegetable fat, nothing to do with real chocolate at all and best avoided.

**Couverture** (French for 'covering') is a special kind of cooking chocolate used by professional chefs. The high cocoa butter content (33–44%) gives a free-flowing, glossy chocolate that handles well. Because of its free-flowing nature, couverture is used for dipping and coating and is often used in chocolate fountains. Not all couverture is ready-tempered. It is useful for baking as it melts easily. It comes in various cocoa mass percentages (dark, milk and white).

## PERCENTAGES EXPLAINED

The difference between varieties of chocolate is in the percentage of cocoa solids. 'Cocoa solids' refers to everything that is in a crushed cacao bean, including added cocoa butter. So when the wrapper on a chocolate bar states that it contains 70% cocoa solids, that means that 70% of the bar comes from cacao beans.

Please note, however, that a high percentage of cocoa solids doesn't necessarily mean a strong chocolate flavour: 70% cocoa solids can mean 50% ground beans plus 20% cocoa butter; or 68% ground beans plus 2% cocoa butter. Taste is the only test! The remaining percentage could be sugar, milk, powdered milk (in the case of milk and white chocolate) vanilla and maybe some lecithin. 100% cocoa solids means it is all bean and perhaps some cocoa butter.

As a rough guide, a high percentage of cocoa solids coupled with a relatively high price should guarantee quality chocolate, but nothing will beat the taste test. Good chocolate doesn't come cheap. Always look on the label for a percentage of cocoa solids – if it isn't there, then don't buy the chocolate.

## AMERICAN CHOCOLATE TYPES

In these days of cross-fertilization of recipes and cookery books between the UK and USA, it is important to clarify basic chocolate types and their equivalents. Legislation is slightly different, but this should explain things.

**Unsweetened or baking chocolate** is pure, set cocoa liquor or cocoa solids, very bitter, no sugar.

**Bitter, dark or plain chocolate** contains a minimum of 35% cocoa solids, cocoa butter and sugar.

**Extra bitter chocolate** can contain up to 70% or more cocoa solids.

**Semi-sweet chocolate** contains a minimum of 15–35% cocoa solids, with extra cocoa butter and added sugar.

**Sweet cooking chocolate** contains the same as above, with more sugar.

**Milk chocolate** contains cacao solids (about 10–15%), cocoa butter, milk or powdered milk, sugar and vanilla.

**White chocolate** – see above.

**Decorator's chocolate or confectioner's chocolate** is the same as chocolate-flavoured cake covering (see page 15).

## OTHER CHOCOLATE FORMS

**Callets or pistoles** are small pellets or flat buttons of chocolate made so that they will melt quickly and evenly. These are mainly used by those in the chocolate trade and come in all three chocolate types. Do not confuse these with mass-produced chocolate drops or chips which are designed to hold their shape when baked, and are not the best chocolate.

**Dragées, chocolate balls etc** are shaped chocolate. Dragées are almond- or cocoa bean-shaped and covered with edible gold, silver or any imaginable colour of candy coating. They also come in heart forms and balls and are used for decoration.

## SOME MODERN TERMS EXPLAINED

Chocolate terminology is constantly evolving, and there is no universal legislation as yet, so here are some explanations of frequently used terms in the world of gourmet chocolate.

**Exclusive derivation chocolate** is a broad term used to emphasize the variety or unique provenance of the bean.

**Estate chocolate** is made from beans grown on one plantation, and can be made with more than one variety of bean.

**Single-origin and single-variety chocolate** refers to chocolate made with cacao beans from one country or region only. It does *not* refer to the quality or type of the bean. Single variety simply means that only cacao beans of one variety have been used. The quality is determined by the type of bean and the chocolate-making process itself.

**Grand Cru** is a term borrowed from the wine world. It is used to describe high-quality chocolate made from selected cacao beans from particular geographical regions.

# CHOCOLATE TIPS

## STORING CHOCOLATE

Chocolate and cocoa easily absorb other flavours and odours, so it should be stored tightly wrapped in clingfilm in an airtight container in a cool, dry place – NOT the fridge, which is too cold and full of moisture. Kept at 10°C (50°F), all chocolate should stay in good condition for about a year. If badly stored in hot or humid conditions, the cocoa butter (with rapid temperature change) or the sugar crystals (in the case of humidity) in the chocolate may rise to the surface of the chocolate and become visible as a dull, whitish film, called 'bloom'. The bloom will not affect the taste and it can still be used perfectly well in baking.

Always bring chocolate to room temperature in its wrapping before cooking. This way it will not attract moisture in the air.

Due to the high proportion of milk solids in white and milk chocolate, they do not keep as well as cocoa and dark chocolate.

Dark, milk and white chocolate can be frozen providing they are wrapped tightly and thoroughly so that no air can circulate around the surface of the chocolate, thus drawing in moisture. It should be thawed at room temperature, still tightly wrapped. This is really only a good idea if you live in a very hot country.

## TO MELT CHOCOLATE ON THE HOB

Break, chop or grate the chocolate into small, even-sized pieces and put it in a clean, dry, thick Pyrex or china basin. The smaller you chop or grate the chocolate, the easier it will be to melt. Fill a saucepan one-quarter full of hot water and bring to a simmer (never let the water boil). Fit the bowl snugly into the rim of the saucepan so that it is suspended over the simmering water, and no steam can escape around the sides. The base of the bowl must not touch the water or the chocolate will overheat.

If melting a small quantity of chocolate, remove the saucepan from the heat and leave the chocolate to melt – this way it will not overheat.

For larger quantities, leave the bowl on the saucepan until the chocolate looks melted – gently prod it with the end of a spoon – it may look solid when it has in fact melted.

When melted, remove the bowl or pan from the heat and stir the chocolate gently until it is completely melted. Stir with a wooden spoon or a plastic spatula rather than a metal one, which may cause bubbles to form and the chocolate to seize.

Do not let the temperature of the chocolate rise above 50°C (122°F) – a digital or chocolate thermometer is useful for this.

If water or steam comes into contact with the chocolate, the chocolate will seize, go grainy or turn into a solid mass that will not melt. Do not despair! Pour at least two tablespoons of boiling water into the chocolate and stir gently until the whole mass becomes smooth again. It WILL work but be warned, use this rescued chocolate only for baking – truffle dipping is out!

However, if you melt the chocolate with a lot of water, the chocolate will not seize (see individual recipes).

Always take extra care with white chocolate as it melts at a lower temperature and can easily burn if overheated.

## TO MELT CHOCOLATE IN A MICROWAVE OVEN

These are guidelines only. All microwaves have different power outputs. Many factors affect the melting properties of chocolate – amount of cocoa solids, cocoa butter etc, so this is a very rough guide. Err on the cautious side to begin with.

Break or chop the chocolate into small, even-sized pieces and put it in a clean, dry Pyrex or china bowl – thicker bowls help reduce the risk of over-heating the chocolate.

For small quantities, put the microwave on a LOW or MEDIUM setting. For larger quantities, and only once you become more experienced, use HIGH.

Check the chocolate frequently and gently prod it with the end of a spoon – it may look solid when in fact it has melted. White chocolate will burn more easily so watch it very carefully – in fact I don't really like melting this in the microwave because of the risk of hot spots.

The addition of other ingredients, such as butter or liquid, may shorten the melting time.

Approximate melting times in a 650 watt microwave oven:

50–125 g chopped chocolate on 100% power takes about 2 minutes; on 30% power it takes about 5 minutes.

175–225 g chopped chocolate on 100% power takes about 2–2½ minutes; on 30% power it takes about 6 minutes.

If in doubt, melt the chocolate in 1-minute bursts, giving it a prod every now and then.

# SMALL CAKES
## AND BISCUITS

*These little cakes are light and airy, with a subtle chocolate flavour and a delicate hint of orange blossom – and they have those little mounds on top showing that they have been perfectly cooked. The secret is in using two oven temperatures – hot then cooler – and buttering and flouring the tins really well to prevent them sticking.*

# CHOCOLATE AND ORANGE-BLOSSOM MADELEINES

75 g plain flour, plus extra to dust

35 g unsweetened cocoa

1 teaspoon baking powder

3 large eggs

100 g golden caster sugar (minus 2 tablespoons)

2 tablespoons orange-blossom or acacia honey

1 teaspoon vanilla extract

1 teaspoon orange-flower water

75 g unsalted butter, melted and cooled, plus 50 g, melted, to grease

*a piping bag*

*two 9-hole metal madeleine tins*

MAKES 18 MADELEINES

Sift the flour with the cocoa and baking powder in a small bowl.

In a large bowl, whisk the eggs, sugar, honey, vanilla extract and orange-flower water until pale, thick and foamy, then fold in the flour mixture. Drizzle the butter around the edge of the bowl and fold it in. Spoon the mixture into the piping bag (there is no need for a nozzle). Seal the end with a twist of clingfilm and refrigerate for at least 1 hour or even overnight.

Preheat the oven to 230°C (450°F) Gas 8 or its hottest setting. Meanwhile, using a pastry brush, liberally grease the tins with butter and refrigerate until set, then dust with flour.

Take the piping bag out of the fridge and pipe the mixture into the tins until very nearly full. Bake for exactly 4 minutes, then turn the heat down to 200°C (400°F) Gas 6 and bake for a further 4 minutes.

Remove from the oven. Tap the tins sharply on a work surface to loosen the madeleines and let them tumble out. Leave to cool on a wire rack, then store in an airtight container. Serve with a cup of hot chocolate or Earl Grey tea.

*A good, fudgy brownie is hard to beat. Children might prefer these made with a mild dark chocolate or even a good milk chocolate. Make double quantities of this recipe and freeze half of it – you'll be glad you did.*

# DOUBLE CHOCOLATE AND WALNUT BROWNIES

175 g unsalted butter, softened

400 g golden caster sugar

3 large eggs, beaten

125 g dark chocolate (60–70% cocoa solids)

1 teaspoon vanilla extract

150 g plain flour

150 g walnuts, roughly chopped

200 g white chocolate chips

*a deep 23-cm square baking tin, base-lined with non-stick baking parchment*

MAKES 16 BROWNIES

Preheat the oven to 180°C (350°F) Gas 4.

Using an electric whisk, cream the butter and sugar together until pale and fluffy, then beat in the eggs. Melt the chocolate according to the instructions on page 17. Stir the melted chocolate and vanilla extract into the butter mixture. Fold in the flour, then the walnuts and half the chocolate chips. Spoon into the prepared baking tin and smooth the surface. Scatter with the remaining chocolate chips (these may brown slightly when baked).

Bake for 30–35 minutes or until a cocktail stick inserted into the centre pulls out with fudgy crumbs attached. Do not over-cook as the brownies will continue to cook in the tin when you remove them from the oven. Leave to cool in the tin – this helps keep the brownies moist. When cold, turn out of the tin, peel off the paper and cut into 16 squares. Store in an airtight container.

*Make these muffins to eat straight out of the oven whilst the chocolate is still soft and melting – there won't be any left by the end of the day! You could make them using milk instead of soured cream, but the sponge won't be as soft and crumbly. Pop a paper muffin case into each muffin tin hole before baking and there will be no washing up.*

# WARM CHOCOLATE MUFFINS

Preheat the oven to 200°C (400°F) Gas 6.

Sift the flour, cocoa, baking powder and bicarbonate of soda in a large bowl and stir in the chopped and grated chocolates. In a separate bowl, beat together the eggs, sugar, soured cream and melted butter. Add the liquid mixture to the dry ingredients and stir until just combined and the mixture is fairly stiff. Don't over-mix otherwise the muffins will be tough. Spoon the mixture into the muffin tin holes to fill almost to the tops.

Bake for 20 minutes until risen and firm. Leave in the tin for about 15 minutes before turning out as the mixture is quite tender: cakes made with soured cream or buttermilk have a lovely tender crumb. Turn out onto a wire rack and serve warm or cool.

275 g plain flour

30 g unsweetened cocoa

2½ teaspoons baking powder

½ teaspoon bicarbonate of soda

185 g dark chocolate (60–70% cocoa solids), very roughly chopped

100 g milk chocolate (over 32% cocoa solids), grated

2 large eggs, beaten

100 g light muscovado sugar

300 ml soured cream

100 g unsalted butter, melted

*a 12-hole non-stick muffin tin*

MAKES 12 MUFFINS

*For these little treats, I have taken the basic recipe for one of the most famous chocolate cakes in the world, Viennese Sachertorte, and baked it in small moulds. Instead of sandwiching and covering the cakes with apricot jam, I thought a juicy, candied apricot nestling on top of each one would be really exciting. If you are short of time, use real glacé apricots. A glossy coat of luscious chocolate icing finishes off these little Sachertortes perfectly.*

# LITTLE SACHERTORTES

1 recipe Glossy Chocolate Glaze (page 136)

200 g dark chocolate (60–70% cocoa solids)

125 g unsalted butter, cubed

8 eggs, separated

2 teaspoons vanilla extract

a pinch of salt

175 g golden caster sugar

125 g plain flour

CANDIED APRICOTS
(MAKES ABOUT 300 G)

225 g granulated sugar

2 tablespoons golden syrup

250 g dried apricots (at least 24)

vegetable oil, to grease

*12 dariole moulds, or similar*

MAKES 12 SACHERTORTES

To make the candied apricots, put the sugar and syrup in a heavy-based, wide pan, (at least 8 cm deep) with 175 ml water. Heat gently, stirring occasionally, for about 10 minutes, or until the sugar has completely dissolved. Add the apricots, then turn up the heat and bring to the boil. Turn down the heat to a gentle simmer and cook, uncovered, until the apricots are slightly plump and glassy – about 25 minutes. Baste and turn them occasionally. Remove the pan from the heat, cover tightly and leave to stand for 20 minutes or even overnight to plump up the fruit.

Grease a wire rack lightly with vegetable oil and set on top of a tray or baking sheet. Lift the apricots out of the syrup with a slotted spoon and set on the rack to drain and cool. Reserve the syrup. When the apricots are cold, layer between sheets of non-stick baking parchment in an airtight container. Refrigerate for up to 1 month.

Preheat the oven to 180°C (350°F) Gas 4. Butter and flour the dariole moulds and base-line with circles of non-stick baking parchment.

To make the cake batter, melt the chocolate with the butter according to the instructions on page 17. Lightly beat the egg yolks, then add them to the chocolate mixture with the vanilla extract and beat until smooth.

Using an electric whisk, whisk the egg whites with the salt in a clean, dry bowl until they form stiff peaks, then gradually beat in the sugar to make a stiff meringue mixture. Fold a tablespoon of the meringue into the chocolate mixture with a metal spoon to loosen it, then fold in the rest. Sift the flour on top and fold in gently. Spoon the batter into the moulds and tap them gently on the table to settle the mixture. Put them on a baking sheet and bake for 20–25 minutes, or until a skewer inserted in the centre comes out clean. Remove from the oven and leave to cool in the moulds. When cool, slice off any cake that has risen above the mould to make a flat base. Invert onto a wire rack set on top of a tray and brush with the reserved apricot syrup.

Place two small (or one large) candied apricots on top of each Sachertorte, then spoon the Glossy Chocolate Glaze over each one to cover completely. Refrigerate for 30 minutes to set. Serve at room temperature.

*These are my favourite cakes from a French pâtisserie. I often buy one and take it to a café to eat with a steaming cup of coffee – almost a religious experience! Follow my instructions below for perfect choux pastry. Weigh and measure everything exactly, sift the flour well and don't boil the liquid until the butter has melted. Add the beaten egg gradually: too little and the pastry will not rise properly, too much and the pastry will collapse. The choux buns must dry out completely before filling, so returning them to the oven once pierced will help. Sometimes these are piped decoratively with buttercream icing, but I prefer them quite plain. Once cool, the buns can be used immediately, stored in an airtight container or frozen.*

# RELIGIEUSES AU CHOCOLAT

1 recipe Chocolate Crème Pâtissière (page 137), at room temperature

½ recipe Glossy Chocolate Glaze (page 136), warmed

165 g plain flour

a good pinch of salt

125 g unsalted butter, cubed

125 ml milk

4 medium eggs, beaten

*a piping bag fitted with a plain, medium nozzle*

MAKES 6 RELIGIEUSES

Preheat the oven to 190°C (375°F) Gas 5.

Sift the flour with the salt twice onto a large sheet of greaseproof paper.

Put the butter in a heavy-based pan with the milk and 125 ml water and heat slowly. The liquid must not boil until the butter has completely melted. Once at a rolling boil, shoot in the flour all at once, remove the pan from the heat and beat well until all the lumps are gone and the mixture JUST begins to pull away from the sides of the pan. Do not over-beat or the mixture will become heavy and greasy.

Leave to cool for 5 minutes, then using an electric whisk or a food mixer, gradually beat in the eggs, until thickened and glossy. Beat well between each addition – the more you beat at this stage, the lighter the pastry will be. You may not have to add all the egg. The mixture is ready when it is smooth and shiny, still holds its shape and will reluctantly leave the spoon when tapped. Spoon into the piping bag.

Wet two heavy baking sheets and pipe 6 walnut-sized mounds of choux onto one and 6 larger mounds, about 5 cm in diameter, onto the other, spacing the mounds well apart.

Bake for 20–25 minutes for the smaller choux and 35 minutes for the larger ones. They should look well puffed and golden brown. Remove from the oven and make a large hole in the base of each one with the tip of a knife. Replace on the baking sheets and return to the oven for a further 5 minutes to dry out the insides. Leave to cool on a wire rack.

Put the Chocolate Crème Pâtissière into a clean piping bag and pipe into the base hole of each choux. Dip the tops of the filled choux buns into the warm Glossy Chocolate Glaze and leave for 5 minutes to set. Sit each small choux on top of a larger one. You may like to trim the base from the smaller ones to ensure a good fit! Eat immediately before they become soggy.

*These are large, flat cookies, perfect for sandwiching together with ice cream. To make smaller ones for eating with malted milk or a milkshake, use smaller spoonfuls and don't spread the mixture out. Although real chopped chocolate tastes better, it won't hold its shape as nicely as ready-made chocolate chips. For real chocoholics, use cacao nibs instead.*

# DOUBLE CHOCOLATE CHIP COOKIES

75 g unsalted butter, softened

75 g golden caster sugar

75 g light soft brown sugar, sifted

1 large egg, beaten

½ teaspoon vanilla or chocolate extract (see note)

150 g self-raising flour

25 g unsweetened cocoa

¼ teaspoon salt

100 g (or more) dark and white (or milk) chocolate chips (or roughly chopped chocolate)

*a heavy, non-stick baking sheet*

MAKES ABOUT 12 LARGE COOKIES

Preheat the oven to 180°C (350°F) Gas 4.

Using an electric whisk, cream the butter and sugars together until pale and fluffy. Beat in the egg and vanilla extract.

Sift the flour with the cocoa and salt in a small bowl. Fold into the egg mixture with the chocolate chips.

Place 4 heaped tablespoonfuls of the mixture on the prepared baking sheet, spacing them well apart. Press down and spread out to about 5 mm thick with the back of a wet spoon or with dampened fingers (you may like to scatter some more chocolate chips over the top). Bake for 10–12 minutes. Leave to cool on the baking sheet for 1 minute, then transfer to a wire rack. When cool, store in an airtight container. Repeat with the remaining mixture.

**Note:** Chocolate extract is a fat-free flavouring made by the alcoholic extraction from a blend of natural cacao beans. Star Kay White's Pure Chocolate Extract is imported from the USA by G. Costa and Co Ltd, Aylesford, Kent ME20 7NA; telephone 01622 717777.

*Ballet dancer Anna Pavlova and opera singer Dame Nellie Melba were so loved by their public that both had sweet dishes named after them. Actress Sarah Bernhardt captured hearts wherever she appeared and was similarly honoured by a Danish chef who concocted and named these delectable cakes in her honour.*

# SARAH BERNHARDT CAKES

2 recipes Chocolate Ganache (page 136), at room temperature

1 recipe Glossy Chocolate Glaze (page 136)

100 g ground almonds

100 g golden caster sugar

1 large egg white, lightly beaten

½ teaspoon bitter almond extract

gold leaf or finely chopped pistachios, to decorate

*a heavy baking sheet, lined with non-stick baking parchment*

*a piping bag fitted with a plain, 2-cm nozzle*

MAKES 20 CAKES

Put the ground almonds and sugar in a blender and process until finely ground. Tip into a bowl and beat in the egg white and almond extract until you get a smooth, workable paste.

Put the mixture into the piping bag and pipe twenty 4-cm mounds onto the prepared baking sheet, spacing them at least 2.5 cm apart. Leave to stand for 30 minutes.

Preheat the oven to 150°C (300°F) Gas 2.

Bake the macaroons for about 20 minutes, or until they turn pale beige. Slip the paper and macaroons onto a wire rack to cool. When cool, lift the macaroons off the paper and store in an airtight container for up to 3 days.

Beat the Chocolate Ganache until the colour lightens and it becomes stiff enough to hold its shape. Do not over-beat. Spoon the ganache into a clean piping bag and nozzle. Pipe a 5-cm high teardrop on top of each macaroon, covering the base completely. Chill (or even freeze) for at least 1 hour.

Strain the Glossy Chocolate Glaze through a fine strainer to remove any bubbles. Leave to cool until almost cold but still runny – about 30 minutes. Pour into a warm wide-necked jug or deep bowl. Holding the cake by the base, dip the chilled ganache part quickly and evenly into the glaze. The glaze should cover the join between the ganache and macaroon. Sit each cake on its base, then sprinkle with flecks of gold leaf or finely chopped pistachios. Cover and refrigerate until ready to serve. These can be made up to 2 days in advance.

# CAKES AND TEABREADS

*There's something about the combination of really dark chocolate and bitter cherries that is beguiling. These moist little teabreads are studded with those succulent cherries in syrup often found spooned over ice cream in Italian ice cream parlours. More often than not they are sold in lovely blue-and-white jars, but I seek out the cheaper tins from Italian delis. Creamy white macadamia nuts are full of oil that can turn rancid very quickly, so don't let them hang around the storecupboard for too long – use them in these teabreads instead.*

# CHOCOLATE, CHERRY AND MACADAMIA TEABREADS

300 g plain flour

50 g unsweetened cocoa

3 teaspoons baking powder

½ teaspoon bicarbonate of soda

½ teaspoon salt

350 ml milk

100 g amarena cherries, plus 100 ml of their syrup

75 g soft light brown sugar

50 g unsalted butter, softened

100 g dark chocolate (60–70% cocoa solids), broken into pieces

150 g macadamia nuts, roughly chopped, plus extra to scatter

*eight 9-cm loaf tins or two 450-g loaf tins*

MAKES 8 MINI TEABREADS
OR 2 LARGE TEABREADS

Preheat the oven to 150°C (300°F) Gas 2. Grease the loaf tins, base-line with non-stick baking parchment and dust with flour.

Sift the flour, cocoa, baking powder, bicarbonate of soda and salt together in a large bowl.

Heat the milk, amarena cherry syrup, sugar, butter and chocolate together in a medium pan until melted and smooth. Stir this into the flour mixture as quickly and deftly as possible until just combined – as if you were making muffins. Stir in the cherries and macadamia nuts, then spoon into the tins and smooth the surface. Scatter with extra macadamia nuts.

Bake for about 30 minutes for the smaller tins and 1 hour for the larger tins, or until firm. A metal skewer inserted into the centre should come out clean. Remove from the oven and leave to cool in the tins for 10 minutes. Turn out onto a wire rack and leave to cool completely. Store in an airtight container for 1 day to mature before serving.

*This is a real treat for children everywhere or the big kid that lurks in all of us. I like to use milk chocolate and a flavoured yoghurt for children or really dark chocolate and natural yoghurt for adults. This really does improve with keeping – even for a day – but I can never keep my hands off it. I employ the 'stealthy sliver method', and before I know it, it has all gone!*

# CHOCOLATE AND BANANA TEABREAD

55 g unsalted butter, softened

150 g soft light brown sugar

2 large eggs, beaten

100 g natural, banana or chocolate yoghurt

350 g bananas, mashed

300 g self-raising flour

½ teaspoon salt

200 g dark chocolate (60–70% cocoa solids) or milk chocolate (over 32% cocoa solids), grated

chocolate and hazelnut spread, to serve (optional)

*two 450-g loaf tins*

MAKES 2 LARGE LOAVES

Preheat the oven to 180°C (350°F) Gas 4. Grease the loaf tins, base-line with non-stick baking parchment and dust with flour.

Using an electric whisk, beat the butter and sugar together until well mixed (it won't look very creamy). Gradually whisk in the eggs, little by little, then the yoghurt, and finally stir in the mashed bananas. Fold in the flour and salt, then the grated chocolate. Spoon into the tins and smooth the surface.

Bake for about 35 minutes, or until risen and firm. It will crack on the top. A metal skewer inserted into the centre should come out clean. Remove from the oven and leave to cool in the tin for 10 minutes. Turn out onto a wire rack and leave to cool completely. Store in an airtight container for 1 day to mature before serving in thick slices with chocolate and hazelnut spread if you're feeling particularly indulgent!

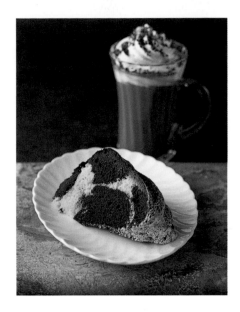

*My first taste of this rich, buttery cake was in the candy-pink, marbled interior of an Austrian coffee shop in the fairytale city of Salzburg. These cakes are piled high in cake shop windows and have that distinctive rounded wobbly base. The marbling effect is easy to achieve – just dollop in large spoonfuls of each mixture randomly and the effect will bake through the cake. And in case you are wondering, two tablespoons of cocoa is plenty – it is very dark when baked.*

# MARBLED BUTTER GUGELHUPF

200 g unsalted butter, softened

200 g golden caster sugar

3 large eggs, beaten

75 ml milk

200 g plain flour

1 teaspoon baking powder

2 tablespoons unsweetened cocoa

icing sugar, to dust

*a 20.5-cm Gugelhupf mould, greased and dusted with flour*

SERVES 6–8

Preheat the oven to 180°C (350°F) Gas 4.

Using an electric whisk, beat the butter and sugar together in a large bowl until pale and fluffy. Add the eggs little by little, beating well between each addition. Beat in the milk.

Sift the flour and baking powder together onto a sheet of greaseproof paper, then shoot it into the creamed mixture and beat until smooth.

Divide the batter in half. Beat the cocoa into one half of the batter. Spoon alternate large spoonfuls of batter into the prepared Gugelhupf mould. Smooth the surface.

Bake for 50–60 minutes, or until the cake springs back when gently pressed in the middle. Remove from the oven and leave to cool in the mould for 10 minutes. Turn out onto a wire rack and leave to cool completely. Dust the top of the Gugelhupf generously with icing sugar.

*For ginger fans only! Chocolate and ginger is one of the best flavour combinations I know. If you are making this for a really decadent treat, use chocolate-coated stem ginger instead of the usual pieces in syrup, and don't cut them up – when the gingerbread is cooked and sliced you will reveal glowing chunks of ginger enrobed with chocolate. Keep it in a tin for a couple of days to give the gingerbread its stickiness. For special occasions I scatter the top with pieces of crystallized ginger.*

# STICKY CHOCOLATE GINGERBREAD

275 g black treacle or molasses

175 g dark chocolate (60–70% cocoa solids), grated

225 g plain flour

2 teaspoons ground ginger

a pinch of salt

150 g whole pieces preserved stem ginger, drained and roughly chopped

125 g unsalted butter, softened

125 g dark muscovado sugar, sifted (to remove lumps)

2 medium eggs, beaten

½ teaspoon bicarbonate of soda

2 tablespoons milk, warmed

extra-large crystallized ginger pieces, to scatter (optional)

*a deep 18-cm square cake tin or 20.5 x 16 x 6.5-cm oval cake tin*

MAKES AN 18-CM SQUARE CAKE
OR A 20.5-CM OVAL CAKE

Preheat the oven to 160°C (325°F) Gas 3. Grease and line the base and sides of the cake tin with non-stick baking parchment.

Put the treacle in a small pan and heat gently until hot, but do not allow it to boil. Remove the pan from the heat and add the chocolate. Stir until melted.

Sift the flour, ground ginger and salt together in a bowl. Add the stem ginger and toss it around in the flour until every piece is coated.

Using an electric whisk, cream the butter and sugar in a large bowl. Beat in the eggs, then the treacle and chocolate mixture, and finally the flour mixture. Dissolve the bicarbonate of soda in the milk and gradually beat this into the batter.

Pour into the prepared cake tin, scatter with the crystallized ginger, if using, and bake for 45 minutes. Reduce the oven temperature to 150°C (300°F) Gas 2 and bake for a further 30 minutes. (If using the oval tin, cook for about 45 minutes at the higher temperature, then about 1 hour at the lower temperature as it will be deeper.) A metal skewer inserted into the centre should come out clean. Leave to cool for 5 minutes in the tin, then turn out onto a wire rack and leave to cool completely. When cold, store in an airtight container for at least a couple of days to mature and become sticky. Don't worry if it sinks a bit in the middle – this is normal.

*I have always wanted to make devil's food cake really devilish by adding the warmth of chilli to the cake mix and icing. I tasted all sorts of chilli-chocolate combinations and found pasilla chilli (also known as 'little raisin') to be the best match. It was mild and fruity and the baked cake became strangely addictive. I couldn't resist making candied fresh chillies for the red devil horn decorations – very edible if a little hot!*

# DEVIL'S FOOD CAKE WITH CHILLI FUDGE ICING

200 g dark chocolate (60–70% cocoa solids)

200 g unsalted butter, softened

350 g soft dark brown sugar

3 eggs, beaten

325 g self-raising flour

2 tablespoons unsweetened cocoa

2 tablespoons pasilla chilli powder (see page 143)

200 ml soured cream

CANDIED CHILLI HORNS

450 g sugar

20 fresh long red chillies

CHILLI FUDGE ICING

100 g unsalted butter, cubed

250 g soft light brown sugar

150 g dark chocolate (60–70% cocoa solids), broken into pieces

1 tablespoon pasilla chilli powder (see page 143)

4 tablespoons single cream

400 g golden icing sugar, sifted

*two deep 18-cm cake tins with removable bases*

SERVES 8–12

To make the candied chilli horns, put the sugar and 600 ml water in a large pan. Bring to the boil for 1 minute. Pierce each chilli near the stalk end and add to the sugar syrup. Bring to the boil, then turn down the heat and simmer for 45 minutes, or until the chillies are translucent and the syrup looks thick and reduced. Turn off the heat and leave to soak in the syrup for 24 hours, if possible. Lift the chillies out of the syrup with a fork, drain well and arrange on non-stick baking parchment. Store in layers in an airtight container for up to 1 month.

Preheat the oven to 180°C (350°F) Gas 4.

Lightly grease the cake tins, dust with flour and base-line with non-stick baking parchment.

To make the cake, melt the chocolate with 200 ml water according to the instructions on page 17. Using an electric whisk, cream the butter and sugar in a large bowl until light and fluffy, then gradually beat in the eggs. Beat in the chocolate mixture. Sift the flour, cocoa and chilli powder onto the mixture and fold in. Fold in the soured cream until smooth. Spoon the batter into the prepared tins and bake for about 30 minutes, or until the cakes begin to wrinkle at the sides of the tins and a skewer inserted into the centre comes out clean. Remove the cakes from the oven and leave to cool completely in the tins. Turn out and remove the paper. Slice each cake across the middle.

To make the chilli fudge icing, put the butter, soft brown sugar, chocolate, chilli powder and cream in a medium pan. Heat very gently, without boiling, until melted and dissolved, then bring to a rolling boil and boil for 3 minutes. Remove from the heat and carefully beat in the icing sugar. Beat well until smooth and thick enough to spread – about 2 minutes. Working quickly, sandwich some icing between layers of cake and pile into a high tower, then spread the remaining icing all over the top and sides.

Trim the candied chillies into 6-cm lengths and push into the icing around the top rim of the cake. It may be tricky to cut, but it looks and tastes fabulous!

*An oldie but a goodie – you never really tire of this moist, rich chocolate dessert. It is really a cooked chocolate mousse, and without a hint of flour. Covering the roulade with a damp tea towel stops it from drying as it cools, keeping it moist and squashy. Serve with the orange compote.*

# ORANGE CHOCOLATE ROULADE

4 tablespoons orange liqueur

icing sugar and golden caster sugar, to dust

300 ml double cream

ORANGE CHOCOLATE ROULADE

225 g dark chocolate (60–70% cocoa solids)

1 teaspoon instant coffee granules

finely grated zest of 1 unwaxed orange (reserving the orange)

5 large eggs, separated

150 g golden caster sugar

CANDIED ZEST

3 large, firm unwaxed oranges (if you can only get waxed, scrub them in hot soapy water before using)

100 g golden caster sugar

*a 23 x 33-cm Swiss roll tin, lined with baking parchment*

SERVES 6

Preheat the oven to 220°C (425°F) Gas 7.

To make the orange chocolate roulade, melt the chocolate with the coffee and orange zest and 4 tablespoons water, according to the instructions on page 17. Stir until smooth. Whisk the egg yolks and sugar in a large bowl until pale and light. Stir in the chocolate mixture. Using an electric whisk, whisk the egg whites in a clean, dry bowl until stiff but not dry. Fold into the chocolate mixture using a metal spoon. Pour into the prepared tin and spread evenly. Bake for 12–15 minutes, or until risen and firm but not dry. Remove from the oven, cover with a damp tea towel and leave to cool in the tin.

To make the candied zest, pare the zest from the oranges in long curling strips, leaving behind any bitter white pith. Reserve the oranges. Blanch the zest in a small pan of boiling water for about 2 minutes, then drain. Put the sugar and 200 ml water in a small pan and heat until the sugar has dissolved. Bring to the boil, then boil for 1 minute. Add the zest and simmer for 25 minutes until it is opaque and the syrup is reduced. Lift out the zest with a fork and leave to dry on a wire rack set over some kitchen paper. Reserve the syrup.

To make the orange compote, cut away the pith and zest from the 4 oranges you have reserved and cut out the segments in-between the membrane. Put these in a bowl with the orange liqueur and reserved syrup. Stir, cover and refrigerate until needed.

Dust a large sheet of greaseproof paper with icing sugar and caster sugar and turn the baked roulade out onto it. Peel the lining paper away and trim the edges of the roulade to neaten. Whip the cream softly and spread over the roulade. Roll up from the shorter side. Don't worry if it cracks – this is normal and just makes it look better! Lift the roulade onto a serving plate. Dust with extra icing sugar and caster sugar. Decorate with the candied orange zest and chill until ready to serve with the orange compote.

*This romantically named classic French cake is all that you expect the enigmatic Queen of Sheba, who stole the heart of King Solomon, to have been – rich, dark and tempting. Veiled in darkest cocoa, adorned with gold dragées and strewn with deep geranium petals, the cake reveals a soft, moist centre – what more can I say? On the practical side, don't over-cook the cake otherwise it will be too dry.*

# QUEEN OF SHEBA CHOCOLATE AND ALMOND CAKE

100 g dark chocolate (60–70% cocoa solids)

100 g unsalted butter, softened

100 g golden caster sugar, plus 1 tablespoon

2 tablespoons rum or coffee

¼ teaspoon bitter almond extract

3 eggs, separated

50 g ground almonds

a pinch of salt

50 g plain flour

2 tablespoons unsweetened cocoa, plus extra to dust

golden chocolate dragées, to decorate

fresh geranium petals, to decorate

*a 20.5-cm normal or springform cake tin, about 4 cm deep*

SERVES 6–8

Preheat the oven to 180°C (350°F) Gas 4. Grease the cake tin, base-line with non-stick baking parchment and dust with flour.

Melt the chocolate according to the instructions on page 17. Using an electric whisk, cream the butter and sugar in a large bowl until really pale and fluffy, then beat in the rum and almond extract followed by the egg yolks, one by one. Working quickly, fold the melted chocolate into the egg mixture, then stir in the ground almonds.

Using an electric whisk, whisk the egg whites with the salt in a clean, dry bowl until they form floppy peaks, then sprinkle in the remaining tablespoon of sugar and whisk again until the mixture forms stiff peaks. Beat a spoonful into the chocolate mixture with a metal spoon to loosen it, then fold in half of the egg whites. Sift the flour and cocoa onto the mixture, then gently fold in. Finally, fold in the remaining egg whites.

Pour the mixture into the cake tin, spreading it out evenly over the base. Bake for 20–25 minutes. Check it after 20 minutes – the cake should be risen and a bit wobbly in the centre, but firm around the edges. Remove from the oven and leave to cool in the tin for 10 minutes. Loosen the sides with a knife and turn out onto a wire rack to cool completely. When cold, dust the top evenly with cocoa and decorate with the gold dragées and geranium petals.

The cake improves with keeping – store in an airtight container for up to 4 days, without decoration.

*A pretty and truly scrumptious, tender cake that benefits from using the best white chocolate you can find. Check on the wrapper that it contains only cocoa butter, sugar and milk solids and no other fat – this way you will get the best flavour. If you are pushed for time, dry the rose petals out in an oven set to the very lowest fan setting and leave the oven door slightly ajar.*

# WHITE CHOCOLATE MASCARPONE CAKE

3–4 tablespoons raspberry liqueur or raspberry vodka (optional)

CRYSTALLIZED ROSE PETALS

1 egg white

petals of 2 white or cream roses, rinsed and dried

caster sugar, to sprinkle

CAKE BATTER

100 g white chocolate (over 25% cocoa butter)

175 g unsalted butter, softened

200 g golden caster sugar

3 large eggs, separated, at room temperature

1 teaspoon vanilla extract

250 g self-raising flour

100 ml buttermilk or soured cream

CREAMY WHITE CHOCOLATE ICING

175 g white chocolate (over 25% cocoa butter)

350 g mascarpone or soft cream cheese (such as Philadelphia), at room temperature

50 g unsalted butter, at room temperature

1 teaspoon vanilla extract

about 300 g icing sugar, sifted

*a pastry brush*

*a 23-cm springform cake tin*

SERVES 8

To crystallize the rose petals, beat the egg white until loosely frothy, then paint onto the rose petals with a pastry brush. Sprinkle with sugar to coat completely, arrange on a cake rack or non-stick baking parchment and leave in a warm place to dry out and crisp – at least overnight. Leave to cool, then store between layers of kitchen paper in an airtight container.

Preheat the oven to 180°C (350°F) Gas 4. Grease the bottom and sides of the cake tin and base-line with non-stick baking parchment. Dust the sides with flour and tap out the excess.

To make the cake batter, melt the chocolate with 100 ml water according to the instructions on page 17. Using an electric whisk, cream the butter and sugar in a large bowl for about 5 minutes until pale and fluffy. Gradually beat in the egg yolks, one at a time, then beat in the melted white chocolate and the vanilla extract. Using a large metal spoon, fold in half of the flour, then the buttermilk, and then the remaining flour. Using a clean electric whisk, whisk the egg whites in a clean, dry bowl until just stiff but not dry. Beat one-third of the beaten egg whites into the cake mixture to loosen it, then carefully fold in the rest.

Spoon the batter into the prepared cake tin. Bake for 35–40 minutes, or until the cake springs back when touched in the centre and a fine skewer inserted in the centre comes out clean. Remove from the oven and leave to cool for 10 minutes in the tin, then turn out onto a wire rack, peel off the lining paper and leave to cool completely.

To make the creamy white chocolate icing, melt the chocolate according to the instructions on page 17 and leave until almost cold. With an electric whisk, beat in the mascarpone, butter and vanilla extract until smooth. Beat in the icing sugar until creamy and spreadable – you may not need it all. Cover and keep at room temperature.

Place the cake on a serving platter and prick all over with a skewer. Spoon over the raspberry liqueur and leave it to soak in for 30 minutes. Spread the icing all over the cake. Refrigerate until needed and scatter with the rose petals just before serving.

# TARTS
## AND PIES

*This is wickedly delicious. Use the darkest chocolate you can find and serve in thin slices. The higher the percentage of cocoa solids in the chocolate, the more intense this is. Use a high-quality chocolate like Amedei Tuscan Black and you won't be disappointed. The filling is gooey and rich and needs nothing more than a dollop of crème fraîche or some pouring cream served with it. I like to add a touch of magic with some edible silver leaf known as varak in India, which is said to have an aphrodisiac effect. The tart case is essentially the classic French sweet pastry, but with a chocolatey twist. It can burn very easily due to the high sugar content, so watch it like a hawk when it is in the oven – time it! This is used for all types of French pâtisserie and tartlets as it holds its shape well when baking and is quite robust when filled.*

# BLACK MAGIC TART

edible silver leaf, to decorate

icing sugar, to dust

crème fraîche, to serve

CHOCOLATE PATE SUCREE

150 g plain flour

50 g unsweetened cocoa

a pinch of salt

75 g golden caster sugar or icing sugar

75 g unsalted butter, cubed,
at room temperature

2 egg yolks

½ teaspoon vanilla extract or chocolate extract

2–3 tablespoons chilled water

FILLING

400 g dark chocolate (60–70% cocoa solids)

125 g unsalted butter, cubed

5 large eggs, separated

125 g golden caster sugar

150 ml double cream, at room temperature

3 tablespoons dark rum or chocolate liqueur

*a 25-cm tart tin, 4 cm deep,
with a removable base*

*baking beans*

*a pastry brush*

SERVES 8

To make the chocolate *pâte sucrée*, sift the flour, cocoa and salt onto a large sheet of greaseproof paper.

Put the sugar, butter, egg yolks and vanilla extract in a food processor and process until smooth. Add the water and process again. Shoot in the ingredients from the greaseproof paper and work until just combined. Turn out onto a lightly floured work surface and knead gently until smooth. Form into a disc and wrap in clingfilm. Refrigerate for at least 30 minutes.

Remove the pastry from the fridge and bring to room temperature before rolling out. Preheat the oven to 190°C (375°F) Gas 5.

Roll the pastry out thinly on a lightly floured work surface – this is quite a delicate pastry to roll so be sure to use enough (but not too much) flour. Use to line the tart tin. Prick the pastry all over with a fork, then refrigerate or freeze for 15 minutes.

Line the tart case with aluminium foil or greaseproof paper, fill with baking beans and bake blind for 15 minutes. Remove the foil and beans, reduce the oven temperature to 180°C (350°F) Gas 4 and return to the oven for 10–15 minutes to dry out and brown – watch it very carefully because it can burn easily. Remove from the oven. (Leave the oven on.)

To make the filling, melt the chocolate with the butter according to the instructions on page 17. Remove the bowl from the heat and leave to cool for about 1 minute.

Put the egg yolks and sugar in a bowl and whisk with an electric whisk until pale and creamy. Stir the cream and rum into the melted chocolate mixture, then quickly fold in the egg yolk mixture. Whisk the egg whites in a clean, dry bowl until soft peaks form. Quickly fold into the chocolate mixture with a metal spoon.

Pour the filling into the pastry case and bake for 20–25 minutes until puffed and a bit wobbly in the centre. Remove from the oven and leave to cool – the filling will sink and firm up as it cools. Decorate by delicately applying silver leaf to the top of the tart with a pastry brush, then dust with icing sugar and serve at room temperature with a dollop of crème fraîche.

*Everyone in Italy knows this fabulous cake filled with chocolate custard cream and topped with crunchy pine nuts. The fragrance of this cake is so evocative that when I bake this in Italy, people seem to crawl out of the woodwork, sniffing the air and asking if there's a Torta del Nonno in the oven.*

# TORTA DEL NONNO (GRANDFATHER'S CAKE)

2 egg yolks, beaten, to glaze

4–6 tablespoons pine nuts

icing sugar, to dust

PASTRY

175 g unsalted butter, softened

100 g golden caster sugar

2 egg yolks

finely grated zest of 1 unwaxed orange

1 teaspoon vanilla extract

a pinch of salt

250 g plain flour

CHOCOLATE CUSTARD FILLING

600 ml milk

50 g dark chocolate (60–70% cocoa solids), finely chopped

2 egg yolks

75 g golden caster sugar

1 tablespoon plain flour, cornflour or potato starch

3 tablespoons unsweetened cocoa

½ teaspoon vanilla extract

*a 22.5-cm tart tin with a removable base*

*baking beans*

*a pastry brush*

SERVES 8

To make the pastry, cream the butter and sugar in a large bowl, using an electric whisk, until light and fluffy. Beat in the egg yolks, orange zest, vanilla extract and salt. Stir in the flour until almost mixed. Transfer to a lightly floured work surface and knead gently until smooth. Divide into two pieces – one slightly bigger than the other. Form into discs, wrap in clingfilm and refrigerate for at least 30 minutes.

Roll out the larger piece of pastry as thinly as possible and use to line the tart tin. Prick the pastry all over with a fork and freeze for at least 15 minutes.

Preheat the oven to 190°C (375°F) Gas 5. Line the tart with aluminium foil or greaseproof paper, fill with baking beans and bake blind for 15 minutes. Remove the foil and baking beans and return to the oven for a further 10 minutes to dry out. Remove from the oven and leave to cool. (Leave the oven on.)

Meanwhile, to make the chocolate custard filling, heat the milk with the chocolate in a large pan. When it is just about to boil, take it off the heat. Whisk the egg yolks with the sugar in a large bowl, then whisk in the flour and cocoa. Whisk in the hot chocolate milk. Return the mixture to the pan and heat gently, stirring until starting to thicken. Once it reaches a very slow boil, simmer for 2 minutes, then stir in the vanilla extract. Pour into the cooled pastry case and leave to cool.

Roll the remaining pastry out to a circle that is slightly larger than the diameter of the tart tin. Brush the rim of the pastry case with the beaten egg yolks and cover the filling with the pastry circle, pressing it firmly against the cooked edges, then trim away the excess. Brush the pastry with more egg yolk and scatter over the pine nuts. Make a couple of air holes in the top. Bake for 1 hour, then remove from the oven and leave to cool completely. Dust with icing sugar and serve.

*This is my variation on the classic Normandy apple and almond tart. Frangipane is the term for an almond-flavoured cream, and in my version here, it has become a soft, chocolatey almond sponge. Pears, chocolate and almonds go so well with each other, especially if you choose pears that are not too ripe and still slightly firm. The ground almonds keep the rich, buttery filling moist. Don't forget to add the chocolate liqueur – it makes this tart truly special.*

# PEAR AND CHOCOLATE FRANGIPANE TART

4 medium, firm pears, unpeeled

150 ml seedless raspberry jam

2 tablespoons Ruby Port

toasted shredded or flaked almonds, to scatter (optional)

single cream, to serve (optional)

PASTRY

250 g plain flour

1 teaspoon salt

125 g unsalted butter, softened

1 large egg yolk

2½–3 tablespoons chilled water

CHOCOLATE FRANGIPANE FILLING

100 g unsalted butter, softened

100 g golden caster sugar

2 eggs, beaten

1–2 tablespoons chocolate liqueur

100 g ground almonds

2 tablespoons unsweetened cocoa

*a shallow 25-cm tart tin with a removable base*

*a pastry brush*

SERVES 8–10

To make the pastry, sift the flour and salt onto a sheet of greaseproof paper. Put the butter and egg yolk in a food processor and blend until smooth. Add the chilled water and blend again. Shoot in the ingredients from the greaseproof paper and blend until just combined. Turn out onto a lightly floured work surface and knead gently until smooth. Form into a disc, wrap in clingfilm and refrigerate for at least 30 minutes. Bring to room temperature before rolling out.

To make the chocolate frangipane filling, put the butter in a large bowl and beat with an electric whisk until creamy. Gradually add the sugar and beat until pale and fluffy. Gradually beat in the eggs and the chocolate liqueur, then stir in the ground almonds and the cocoa. Cover and set aside.

Roll out the pastry on a lightly floured work surface and use to line the tart tin. Prick the pastry all over with a fork and refrigerate until firm.

Preheat the oven to 200°C (400°F) Gas 6, and put a heavy baking sheet on the middle shelf.

Spread the chocolate frangipane evenly over the chilled pastry case.

Halve the pears and scoop out the cores. Cut each half into thirds and arrange them randomly over the chocolate frangipane.

Transfer the tart to the preheated baking sheet and bake for 10–15 minutes, or until the pastry starts to brown. Reduce the heat to 180°C (350°F) Gas 4, and bake for a further 15–20 minutes or until the pears are tender and the frangipane is set. Remove from the oven and transfer to a wire rack to cool.

About 20 minutes before serving, melt the jam with the port in a small pan and boil for 1 minute to make a glaze. Remove the tart from the tin, brush with the glaze, scatter with the almonds, if using, and serve at room temperature – never chilled – with cream, if using.

*What could be more heavenly than a melting, flaky chocolate crust hiding a rich, soft, moist chocolate and almond filling? The ultimate would be made with buttery home-made puff pastry, but if you buy it ready-made, it will save hours! You can leave out the Chocolate Crème Pâtissière if you like – the result will be denser but just as delicious. Always serve this warm, not hot, with pouring cream or Crème Anglaise.*

# CHOCOLATE ALMOND PITHIVIERS

600 g ready-rolled all-butter puff pastry

1 egg yolk, lightly beaten with 1 tablespoon milk, to glaze

30 g icing sugar

pouring cream or Crème Anglaise (page 137), to serve (optional)

CHOCOLATE ALMOND CREAM

60 ml Chocolate Crème Pâtissière (page 137)

65 g unsalted butter, at room temperature

65 g icing sugar, sifted

1 large egg

65 g ground almonds

2 tablespoons unsweetened cocoa

2 tablespoons chocolate liqueur (optional)

50 g dark chocolate (60–70% cocoa solids), grated

*a 20-cm plate or flan ring*

*a 24-cm plate or flan ring*

*a pastry brush*

SERVES 8

To make the chocolate almond cream, cream the butter and icing sugar together with an electric whisk in a medium bowl until pale and fluffy. Gradually beat in the egg, then the ground almonds, cocoa and liqueur, if using. Finally, beat in the Chocolate Crème Pâtissière and the grated chocolate. Set aside.

Divide the puff pastry in two – one slightly bigger than the other (about 350 g and 250 g). To make the base, roll out the smaller piece of pastry directly onto a lightly floured baking sheet, into a rough circle about 26 cm in diameter and 2 mm thick. To make the top, roll out the bigger piece of pastry to a circle of the same diameter, but about 3 mm thick.

Gently press the 20-cm plate or flan ring onto the pastry base, centring it carefully. It should make a light but visible indentation. Spoon the chocolate almond cream into the centre of the pastry base, then spread it evenly within the marked circle. Glaze the exposed pastry edge with some egg-milk wash.

Place the second circle of pastry on top and press around the dome of the chocolate almond cream first to seal it in, then press around the pastry edge. Set the 24-cm plate or flan ring centrally over the pastry and cut all the way around it to make a perfect circle. Discard the excess pastry. Refrigerate the pie for 30 minutes.

Preheat the oven to 240°C (475°F) Gas 10, if possible, or its hottest setting.

Remove the pie from the fridge and, using a small sharp knife, cut the outer rim into a scallop-shaped border. Glaze the entire surface of the pie with egg-milk wash, then, with the point of a knife, score faint curved lines spiralling from the centre of the cake to the edge, like sunrays.

Bake for 10 minutes to set the pastry, then reduce the oven temperature to 200°C (400°F) Gas 6 and bake for a further 25 minutes. Increase the oven temperature to 220°C (425°F) Gas 7. Remove the pie from the oven and sift the icing sugar evenly over the surface. Bake for a further 5 minutes. Serve warm, with pouring cream if you like.

**Note:** You can freeze the pie, unbaked, for up to 1 week. To bake from frozen, leave at room temperature for 30 minutes, then bake while still semi-frozen, allowing an extra 10 minutes in the oven at the 200°C stage.

*A gorgeous fudgy, nutty tart made all the more delicious by the addition of bourbon whiskey. Instead of pecans, you can use a mixture of your favourite nuts, although creamier nuts, such as walnuts, brazils and macadamias are best. Making your own pastry for this will make all the difference – there's nothing to beat a light, crumbly, buttery pastry case. Freeze any leftover pastry to make tartlets – or make little individual tartlets instead for afternoon tea! You can also make this with Chocolate Pâte Sucrée (page 63).*

# CHOCOLATE, BOURBON AND PECAN TART WITH COFFEE BEAN SAUCE

1 recipe Coffee Bean Sauce, flavoured with bourbon (page 137)

RICH SHORTCRUST PASTRY

200 g plain flour

50 g unsweetened cocoa

2 tablespoons icing sugar

½ teaspoon salt

125 g unsalted butter, cubed

2 egg yolks mixed with 2 tablespoons iced water

1 egg, beaten, to glaze

CHOCOLATE NUT FILLING

125 g dark chocolate (60–70% cocoa solids)

50 g unsalted butter, cubed

3 large eggs, beaten

175 ml maple syrup

3 tablespoons bourbon whiskey

250 g pecan nuts

*a 23-cm tart tin*

*baking beans*

SERVES 6

To make the rich shortcrust pastry, sift the flour, cocoa, icing sugar and salt in the bowl of a food processor. Add the butter and process for about 30 seconds until the mixture resembles very fine breadcrumbs. Pour in the egg yolks and iced water and pulse for 10 seconds. The dough should start to come together in large, raggy lumps. If not, add another tablespoon of iced water and pulse again. As soon as the dough forms one big lump (don't over-process or the pastry will be tough), tip out onto a lightly floured work surface and knead lightly into a firm but malleable dough. Shape into a disc, wrap in clingfilm and refrigerate for at least 30 minutes.

Remove the pastry from the fridge and bring to room temperature. Preheat the oven to 190°C (375°F) Gas 5.

Roll the pastry out on a lightly floured work surface and use to line the tart tin. Prick the pastry all over with a fork and refrigerate or freeze for 15 minutes. Line the tart with aluminium foil or greaseproof paper, fill with baking beans and bake blind for 10–12 minutes. Glaze the pastry case with the beaten egg and bake for a further 5–10 minutes. Remove from the oven and leave to cool.

To make the chocolate nut filling, reduce the oven temperature to 160°C (325°F) Gas 3. Melt the chocolate with the butter according to the instructions on page 17. Put the eggs, maple syrup and bourbon in a bowl and beat well. Add to the melted chocolate (still in a bowl over a pan of simmering water). Stir well, and keep stirring over low heat until the mixture starts to thicken. Stir in the pecan nuts and pour into the pastry case.

Bake for 35–40 minutes, or until just set – the filling will still be a bit wobbly.

Serve the tart warm with the Coffee Bean Sauce.

# THE DUTCH AND COCOA

For more than a century after its discovery, the Spanish had the monopoly on cocoa and kept the drink a coveted secret. In 1585, Dutch pirates encountered the precious bean cargo when they plundered a Spanish ship and threw it overboard thinking it was sheep's droppings! Little did they know that the Netherlands would become the world's largest exporter of cocoa products in the twenty-first century.

By the end of the seventeenth century, due to the universal popularity of the hot drink, the Dutch East India Company was growing cacao in the new colony of Surinam (formerly a British colony) and shipping it to be ground in Amsterdam. The trade grew and grew and by the end of the eighteenth century, there were more than 30 chocolate (the drink) factories in Amsterdam. The demand for chocolate was so high that mustard mills were converted into chocolate mills. Chocolate houses were outnumbering coffee houses.

The Dutch chocolate revolution didn't end there. A Dutch doctor, Conraad van Houten, developed a method of pressing, whereby the drink could be greatly improved. Until now, the problem with the hot chocolate drink was that there was always a layer of greasy cocoa butter and scum floating on top. Various methods had been used to absorb the naturally occurring fat. On both sides of the Channel, ground cocoa was experimentally mixed with ground acorns, potato starch, arrowroot and even powdered seashells to make it more palatable. Powdered brick dust, lead-based pigments and rust were added for colour, and analysis commissioned by *The Lancet* in 1851 showed that 90% of brands tested were not pure crushed cacao bean.

In 1828, van Houten came up with two innovations to refine the quality of drinking chocolate and cocoa. Aided by the invention of powerful hydraulic presses in the Industrial Revolution, he patented a method of pressing most of the cocoa butter out of the cocoa liquor to make a cocoa presscake. This was finely ground into almost fat-free cocoa powder, producing a valuable by-product – cocoa butter. He also developed a method to enhance the taste and colour of cacao during the production process through alkalization (the addition of a solution of alkali salt, normally potassium carbonate). This process became known as Dutching (see page 11), and made the cacao less bitter, neutralizing the natural acidity of the bean. Dutched cocoa became milder in taste, with a warmer reddish tint, and when mixed with hot water, it made an infinitely superior drink to its rustic, gritty predecessor.

Today, un-Dutched powdered cocoa is generally described as 'natural' or 'pure', is a much lighter colour, slightly acidic (with a stronger chocolate flavour) and generally not used to make chocolate. I use natural cocoa in recipes which include bicarbonate of soda (an alkali), since combining the two creates a natural raising action that allows the mixture to rise and lighten during baking. I use milder, darker Dutched cocoa for coating truffles and sifting over cakes. The fat content of the cocoa can also affect its colour and is normally between 20–22% (although it is possible to find 15–17% and 10–12%). Fat-free cocoa is not legally called cocoa powder and is mixed with fat, sugar and other ingredients to produce chocolate-flavoured coverings, cake mixes and drinks.

The unique taste and aroma of cocoa is used in many food products to enhance flavour and colour, but it is best-known today for making chocolate.

It is not only the type of bean and the drying process that determine the colour and the taste, but also the manufacturing process (see page 12 for the complete process). It is at the grinding stage that powdered cocoa is obtained. Most cocoa manufacturers can customize their cocoa for individual bulk customers according to their needs, and a variety of colours can be produced by carefully adjusting the pH levels, the moisture content and roasting temperatures and times.

Today, the Netherlands is the world's market leader for cocoa with a share of about 25%. Major outlets are Germany, the USA, France, Italy and Belgium. The Netherlands and France are the most important producers of cocoa butter in Europe, the top buyers being Germany, Belgium, France, the UK and Switzerland. The Netherlands processes 450,000 tons of cacao beans, making it the most important processor in the world. Other major European players are Germany, the UK and France. The average per capita consumption of chocolate in the Netherlands is 5 kg per annum.

*Right: powdered cocoa varies in colour depending on its fat content and whether it has been Dutched*

# HOT PUDDINGS

*There is nothing better on a cold winter's day than the sound (and smell) of a steamed pudding gently rattling in its pan, waiting to be turned out and smothered in custard. This pudding looks good enough to serve at a dinner party, the orange slices glowing out from the dark, sticky sponge. Smaller oranges are best here, and don't peel them – they are cooked, skins and all, for maximum effect. The dates keep the sponge beautifully moist.*

# CHOCOLATE, ORANGE AND DATE STEAMED PUDDING

100 g golden caster sugar

2–3 seedless oranges

200 g unsalted butter, softened

200 g dark muscovado sugar

finely grated zest of 1 unwaxed orange

3 tablespoons fine-cut orange marmalade

3 eggs, beaten

1 tablespoon orange-flower water (optional)

150 g plain flour

50 g unsweetened cocoa

2 teaspoons baking powder

150 g ready-to-eat dates, chopped

custard or Chocolate Crème Anglaise (page 137), to serve

*a 1.2-litre pudding basin*

SERVES 6–8

First make a sugar syrup. Pour 150 ml water into a small saucepan and add the caster sugar. Cook over gentle heat until dissolved.

Slice each orange thinly into about 6 neat slices. Submerge them in the sugar syrup. Set a disc of non-stick baking parchment on top and simmer gently for 30–40 minutes. Lift the oranges out with a slotted spoon and drain on a wire rack. Boil the syrup hard until reduced by half and set aside.

Butter the pudding basin and line the base with a small disc of non-stick baking parchment. Place the best orange slice on top of the disc, and use the rest of the slices to line the sides of the basin.

In a large bowl, cream the butter, muscovado sugar and orange zest using an electric whisk, until light and fluffy. Beat in the marmalade, then gradually beat in the eggs and orange-flower water, if using, mixing very well between each addition. Sift the flour, cocoa and baking powder onto a sheet of greaseproof paper, then fold into the egg mixture. Finally, fold in the dates.

Carefully spoon the pudding mixture into the orange-lined basin. It should come about three-quarters of the way up the sides. Smooth the surface and cover with a disc of non-stick baking parchment. Take a large sheet of aluminium foil and fold it in half. Make a pleat in the centre and place over the basin, with the pleat in the centre. Press the foil over the side of the basin, tie around the top with string and trim away any excess foil. The pleat will open out and allow the pudding to expand during cooking. Stand the basin on a trivet in a large, deep pan and add enough water to come at least 5 cm up the sides. Cover the pan with a lid and simmer gently for 2 hours, topping up the water level from time to time.

Remove the foil and paper disc and insert a small skewer into the centre of the pudding. It should come out clean. If not, re-cover and steam for a little longer. Loosen the pudding around the sides with a thin-bladed knife, turn out onto a warm serving dish and brush with a little of the reserved syrup. Serve with custard or Chocolate Crème Anglaise.

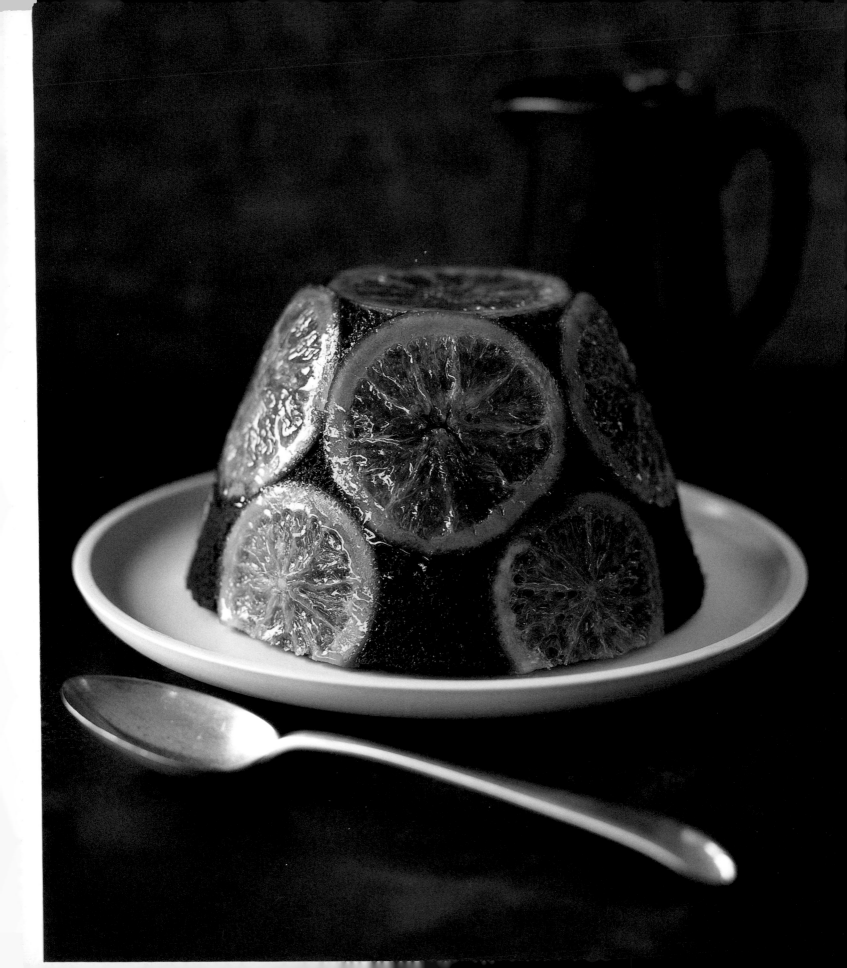

*Italian amarena cherries are addictive. Reserve the drained syrup and stir it into the bitter chocolate sauce. All is not lost if the soufflés collapse – just leave to stand for 5 minutes then turn them out of the ramekins and serve with hot chocolate sauce and whipped cream. I measure my egg whites as a liquid measure for soufflés – it is much more accurate.*

# BLACK FOREST SOUFFLÉ WITH HOT CHOCOLATE SAUCE

Bitter Chocolate Sauce or White Chocolate Sauce (page 135), to serve

300 g dark chocolate (60–70% cocoa solids)

100 g drained amarena cherries

4 egg yolks

250 ml egg whites

100 g golden caster sugar

*6 large ramekins, greased and dusted with sugar*

SERVES 6

Preheat the oven to 220°C (425°F) Gas 7.

Melt the chocolate according to the instructions on page 17. Divide the amarena cherries between the ramekins.

Beat the egg yolks into the melted chocolate with a wooden spoon until the mixture becomes thick and stiff.

Using an electric whisk, whisk the egg whites in a clean, dry bowl until they form soft peaks. Add the sugar and continue to whisk hard for about 3 minutes, or until the whites form soft peaks again and are thick and smooth. Whisk a large tablespoon of the meringue into the chocolate mixture, then carefully fold in the remaining meringue with a metal spoon. It is very important at this stage not to over-fold and knock out the air, as it is the trapped air in the mixture that makes the soufflés rise.

Divide the mixture between the ramekins and give each one a good tap on the work surface to level the top. Set them on a heavy baking sheet.

Bake for 13–15 minutes, or until they are well risen. Serve immediately with Bitter Chocolate Sauce or White Chocolate Sauce. To eat, dig your spoon into the middle of your soufflé and pour in the sauce. Mmmmmmm!

*The pears here absorb the deep, rich flavour of the wine and cinnamon and turn a fabulous colour. I like to put polenta in the cake mix as it gives a lighter texture to the cooked sponge. Always turn this out whilst still warm to reveal the pears in all their glorious stickiness.*

# CHOCOLATE, PORT AND PEAR UPSIDE-DOWN SPONGE

Crème Anglaise (page 137), to serve

6–8 medium under-ripe pears, peeled

1 cinnamon stick

75 g golden caster sugar

150 ml Ruby Port

450 ml full-bodied red wine

CAKE BATTER

100 g plain flour

3 tablespoons unsweetened cocoa

1 teaspoon baking powder

a pinch of salt

75 g polenta

100 g unsalted butter, softened

175 g golden caster sugar

3 large eggs, separated

1 teaspoon vanilla extract

100 ml milk

a 24-cm heavy round cake tin, 5 cm deep, greased

SERVES 6

Halve the pears lengthways and carefully scoop out the core with a teaspoon or melon baller. Put the pears in a wide, shallow sauté pan with the cinnamon and the sugar. Pour over the port and red wine and bring to the boil. Cover and simmer gently for 20 minutes (after which they will still be a little firm). Lift the pears out of the pan with a slotted spoon. Leave to cool. Boil the reserved wine juices hard until well reduced and syrupy.

Arrange the pears cut-side down around the base of the prepared cake tin (wide ends outwards, points towards the middle). Pour over half the wine syrup, reserving the rest. Leave to cool.

Preheat the oven to 190°C (375°F) Gas 5.

To make the cake batter, sift the flour, cocoa, baking powder and salt in a small bowl and stir in the polenta. Using an electric whisk, cream the butter and sugar in a large bowl until pale and fluffy, then beat in the egg yolks and vanilla extract. Fold in the flour mixture, then beat in the milk.

Using an electric whisk, whisk the egg whites in a clean, dry bowl until they form soft peaks. Using a metal spoon, quickly stir a large spoonful of whites into the cake mixture to loosen it, then gently fold in the remainder. Spoon the cake batter over the pears and smooth the surface.

Bake for 45–60 minutes, or until a metal skewer inserted into the centre comes out clean. Remove from the oven and leave to cool for 10 minutes in the tin. Just before serving, put the tin over low heat for 1 minute to warm the pears and help loosen them from the bottom. Run a knife around the edges to loosen the cake and invert onto a warm serving plate. Brush the pears with the reserved syrup. Serve warm or at room temperature with Crème Anglaise.

*Bananas, caramel and chocolate are just one of the world's best combinations – and this uses a lot of bananas! Cutting them up and standing them upright gives a wonderful deep pie that looks amazing. I tried cooking the chocolate with the caramel, but it tended to burn, so I sprinkled it over the hot tart once it was turned out and the effect was divine. Use nice ripe bananas here. If you want to use fewer bananas, cut them in thick diagonal slices and spread out over the base of the pan in a thinner layer.*

# BANANA AND CHOCOLATE TARTE TATIN

Bitter Chocolate Sauce (page 135), whipped cream or Crème Anglaise (page 137), to serve

100 g golden caster sugar

50 g unsalted butter

12 medium, ripe bananas

350 g all-butter puff pastry

75 g dark chocolate (60–70% cocoa solids), finely grated

*a flameproof 25-cm cast-iron frying pan, heavy cake tin or Tatin tin*

SERVES 8

Preheat the oven to 190°C (375°F) Gas 5.

Put the sugar and butter in the cast-iron frying pan, heavy cake tin or Tatin tin. Place over medium heat and cook, stirring every now and then, until the mixture bubbles and turns into a smooth, rich toffee. It will look very grainy to start with and the butter will look as if it has split away from the sugar, but just keep stirring and it will gradually come together. Remove from the heat.

Cut the bananas into 3 even pieces. Arrange them standing upright in the pan or tin, packing them together.

Roll out the pastry on a lightly floured surface into a rough circle 28 cm across. Lay the pastry over the bananas and tuck the edges down into the pan to make the rim of the tart. Prick the top of the pastry here and there with a fork, then bake for 35–40 minutes, or until risen and golden. Remove the pan from the oven and leave to rest for 10 minutes.

Run a sharp knife around the pastry to free the edges. Pour out any caramel liquid that has gathered in the base and reserve. Invert a serving plate over the top of the pan. Carefully turn pan and plate over together, then remove the pan. Pour over the reserved caramel sauce and immediately sprinkle with the grated chocolate and leave to melt in the residual heat. Serve cut into wedges with Bitter Chocolate Sauce, whipped cream or Crème Anglaise.

*Rice pudding must be one of my favourite desserts and is made all the more special by the addition of chocolate and boozy, rum-soaked raisins. I like to spoon the warm raisins over the creamy rice pudding, but you could always cook them in the pudding after they have been well and truly steeped in the rum.*

# CHOCOLATE, RUM AND RAISIN RICE PUDDING

100 g raisins

150 ml dark rum

1 vanilla pod, split lengthways

300 ml milk

300 ml evaporated milk

100 g dark chocolate (60–70% cocoa solids), chopped or grated

50 g pudding rice

*a 900-ml ovenproof dish*

SERVES 4

Preheat the oven to 150°C (300°F) Gas 2.

Put the raisins and rum in a small pan and bring to the boil. Remove from the heat and transfer to a jar or bowl and cover. Leave to soak for at least 3 hours or overnight. This can be done days ahead. Store the raisins in a tightly covered jar in the fridge.

Put the vanilla pod, milk and evaporated milk in a medium pan and bring slowly to the boil. Stir in the chocolate and rice. Stir until the chocolate has melted, then pour into the ovenproof dish. Bake for about 3 hours or until a brown skin forms on top and the rice is cooked and creamy. (Alternatively, if you don't like the skin on traditional rice pudding, simmer very slowly on top of the stove for about 1 hour until thick and creamy.)

To serve, put the soaked raisins and their liquid into a small pan and warm them through. Serve the raisins spooned over the rice pudding.

# CHILLED DESSERTS

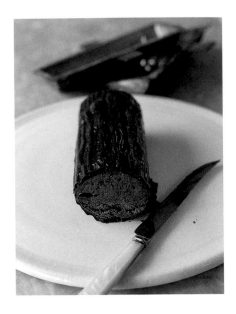

125 g skinned hazelnuts

125 g dark chocolate (60–70% cocoa solids), plus extra to decorate

600 ml double cream

2 eggs, separated

175 g icing sugar

*8 individual ice-cream or jelly moulds*

*a freezerproof tray*

SERVES 8 GENEROUSLY

*A semifreddo is an ice cream made with a meringue base, and it will usually hold its shape even after thawing. When frozen, the mixture is soft enough to cut through with a hot knife. This is best made in little moulds then turned out and decorated with chocolate. However, I have also made it in a traditional Bûche de Noël ice-cream mould (found in a French antique shop) which I first lined with melted chocolate then filled with semifreddo. It looked wonderful – see the picture on the left.* Gianduja *is a chocolate and hazelnut mixture famously from Piemonte in Italy.*

# GIANDUJA SEMIFREDDO

Preheat the oven to 190°C (375°F) Gas 5.

Put the hazelnuts on a baking sheet and roast in the oven for about 8 minutes, or until golden brown. Remove from the oven and leave to cool completely, then grind very finely in an electric spice grinder.

Melt the chocolate according to the instructions on page 17. Reserve the pan of warm water off the heat.

Whisk the cream until it just holds its shape, then fold in the hazelnuts. In a large bowl, whisk the egg yolks with 2 tablespoons of the icing sugar until pale and creamy. Stir the melted chocolate into the egg yolk mixture, then set over the reserved pan of warm water to keep from setting.

Working quickly, whisk the egg whites in a clean, dry bowl until they form floppy peaks. Add the remaining icing sugar, a spoonful at a time, whisking between each addition, until very thick. Fold the hazelnut cream into the chocolate mixture, then fold in the meringue mixture with a metal spoon.

Spoon the mixture into the moulds and smooth the surface. Place a circle of non-stick baking parchment over each one, set on a freezerproof tray and freeze for about 12 hours. Alternatively, freeze in a larger container to serve in scoops. Transfer to the fridge for 10 minutes to soften before serving.

To serve, dip the moulds in a basin of warm water for 10 seconds, then, if the moulds are plastic, give a gentle squeeze and the semifreddos should pop out. If the moulds are metal, slip a thin-bladed knife down one side to loosen. Invert onto chilled plates. To decorate, melt some dark chocolate and pipe it in swirling filigree patterns over non-stick baking parchment. Refrigerate for a couple of minutes, then break the filigree into pieces and use to decorate the semifreddo. Alternatively, decorate with chocolate shavings, curls or thin squares of chocolate.

**Variation:** Brush the inside of a metal ice-cream mould with melted chocolate, making sure it's not too thick. Refrigerate until set. Spoon the cold semifreddo mixture into the mould and smooth the surface. Cover with non-stick baking parchment and freeze for at least 12 hours. Place a plate on the base of the mould, turn upside down and give a sharp tap on the work surface – the chocolate shrinks as it freezes and the whole thing will pop out.

*What a combination – the sorbet is rich, soft, smooth and dark and the ice cream is velvety and voluptuous with the occasional crunch of macadamia nuts. This is a dreamy, creamy ice cream which relies entirely on using the best-quality white chocolate you can buy, otherwise the flavour will suffer. It is the cocoa butter in the white chocolate that gives it a mild chocolate taste, so make sure it contains more than 25% cocoa butter.*

# CHOCOLATE SORBET WITH WHITE CHOCOLATE AND MACADAMIA ICE CREAM

### CHOCOLATE SORBET

250 g golden caster sugar

65 g best-quality unsweetened cocoa, sifted

75 g dark chocolate (60–70% cocoa solids), grated

2 teaspoons vanilla extract

1 teaspoon instant espresso coffee powder

MAKES ABOUT 900 ML

### WHITE CHOCOLATE AND MACADAMIA ICE CREAM

750 ml double cream

250 ml whole milk (or evaporated milk)

175 g best-quality white chocolate (over 25% cocoa butter), chopped

4 egg yolks

150 g golden caster sugar

150 g macadamia nuts, roughly chopped, plus extra to serve

MAKES ABOUT 1.25 LITRES

*an ice-cream maker (optional)*

*a freezerproof tray or container*

*stemmed glasses, chilled*

To make the chocolate sorbet, put 500 ml water, the sugar and cocoa in a pan and whisk well to mix. Bring slowly to the boil, stirring until the sugar has dissolved. Boil fast for 5 minutes to make a thin chocolate syrup. Remove from the heat, add the chocolate, vanilla extract and espresso powder and stir until melted. Leave to cool, then refrigerate.

If using an ice-cream maker, churn-freeze the chilled mixture in two batches. This will take 20–30 minutes. It will increase in volume as it thickens and freezes. Stop churning when thick and smooth, then transfer to a chilled freezerproof tray, cover and freeze. If you don't have an ice-cream maker, put the mixture in a freezerproof tray or container and freeze until it is frozen around the edges. Mash well with a fork and return to the freezer. Continue mashing with a fork and freezing the mixture until thick and smooth, about 2 hours. Transfer to the fridge to soften for 10–15 minutes before serving. The sorbet will be quite soft when fully frozen due to the high quantity of sugar.

To make the white chocolate and macadamia ice cream, put the cream and milk in a pan and bring to the boil. Add the chocolate and stir until melted.

Using an electric whisk, whisk the egg yolks and sugar together until pale and fluffy. Pour the chocolate milk onto the egg mixture, stirring all the time until well blended. Return to the pan and cook over gentle heat for 5 minutes, or until slightly thickened – do not allow to get too hot or it will curdle. Remove from the heat and leave to cool, stirring from time to time until cold.

Churn-freeze in an ice-cream maker or put in the freezer, as above. When smooth and thick, stir in the macadamia nuts. Transfer to the fridge to soften for 20 minutes before serving.

To serve, put a scoop of sorbet, then a scoop of ice cream in each glass and scatter with chopped macadamia nuts.

*My sister Jacks is crazy about the Alps and anything alpine, and found a cake tin in Paris that looks like a mountain range. That was my inspiration here – to make an ice cream to suit an alpine mould. What could be more perfect than an ice cream that tastes of smooth, creamy Swiss milk chocolate studded with white nougat, resembling a triangular Swiss chocolate bar? This truly is a gorgeous ice cream with a satin-like texture interrupted by melting honeyed, nutty nougat. One scoop is not enough. Serve with white chocolate sauce to resemble snowy slopes. Kids go mad for this!*

# SWISS MOUNTAIN ICE CREAM

White Chocolate Sauce (page 135)

500 ml whole milk

250 ml sweetened condensed milk

150 g granulated sugar

2 tablespoons unsweetened cocoa

400 g best-quality milk chocolate
(over 32% cocoa solids), chopped

1 teaspoon vanilla extract

375 ml whipping or double cream, chilled

200 g white nougat, roughly chopped

*an ice-cream maker (optional)*

*a freezerproof tray or container*

*a mountain-shaped mould (optional)*

MAKES ABOUT 2 LITRES

Put the milk, condensed milk, sugar and cocoa in a pan, bring to the boil, then simmer gently for 5 minutes, stirring constantly. Stir in the chocolate and leave to melt, stirring occasionally. Leave to cool completely, then add the vanilla extract and refrigerate for about 1 hour.

Stir the cream into the mixture, then churn-freeze in an ice-cream maker in two batches. This will take 20–30 minutes. It will increase in volume as it thickens and freezes. Stop churning when thick and smooth, add the nougat and churn to mix, then transfer to a chilled freezerproof tray, cover and freeze. If you don't have an ice-cream maker, put the mixture in a freezerproof tray or container and freeze until it is frozen around the edges. Mash well with a fork and return to the freezer. Continue mashing with a fork and freezing the mixture until thick and smooth, about 2 hours. Stir in the nougat. At this stage you can pack it into a mould and return to the freezer.

If the ice cream is in a mould, remove from the freezer and dip briefly in hot water to melt the outside. Invert onto a chilled plate, lifting off the mould. If the ice cream is in a container, transfer to the fridge to soften for 20 minutes before serving in scoops. Drizzle with hot White Chocolate Sauce and serve.

*This is just about the richest, most luscious ice cream you will ever taste, conjuring up childhood memories of hot drinks by the open fire. In fact, malted ice cream is a very American thing, and topped with a hot fudge sauce, it shoots off the superlative scale. Don't use your very best dark chocolate for this – it will be wasted.*

# MALTED CHOCOLATE ICE CREAM WITH RICH CHOCOLATE SAUCE

Rich Chocolate Fudge Sauce (page 135)

300 ml double cream

300 ml milk

100 g instant malted drink powder (such as Ovaltine, Horlicks or Bournvita)

75 g dark chocolate (60–70% cocoa solids), grated

6 egg yolks

175 g golden caster sugar

2–3 tablespoons chocolate liqueur (optional)

*an ice-cream maker (optional)*

*a freezerproof tray or container*

SERVES 6–8 (MAKES 900 ML)

Put the cream and milk in a pan and bring to the boil. Remove from the heat and whisk in the malted powder. Add the chocolate and stir until melted.

Using an electric whisk, whisk the egg yolks and sugar together until pale and fluffy. Pour in the malt mixture, stirring all the time until well blended. Return to the pan and cook for 5 minutes, or until slightly thickened – do not allow to get too hot or it will curdle. Remove the pan from the heat and leave to cool, stirring from time to time until cold. Add the liqueur, if using.

If using an ice-cream maker, churn-freeze the mixture in two batches. This will take 20–30 minutes. It will increase in volume as it thickens and freezes. Stop churning when thick and smooth, then transfer to a chilled freezerproof tray, cover and freeze. If you don't have an ice-cream maker, put the mixture in a freezerproof tray or container and freeze until it is frozen around the edges. Mash well with a fork and return to the freezer. Continue mashing with a fork and freezing the mixture until thick and smooth, about 2 hours. Transfer to the fridge to soften for 20 minutes before serving.

Serve in generous scoops, drizzled with Rich Chocolate Fudge Sauce.

*Reserve your best white, milk and dark chocolates for this dessert. The custards are silky smooth when baked to perfection – don't rush them or raise the temperature otherwise the consistency will be ruined. For an even richer custard, use double cream instead of the milk-cream combination.*

# THREE LITTLE CHOCOLATE POTS

350 ml milk

350 ml single cream

2 tablespoons golden caster sugar

4 large egg yolks

2 eggs

1 teaspoon vanilla extract

50 g white chocolate (over 25% cocoa butter), grated

50 g milk chocolate (over 32% cocoa solids), grated

50 g dark chocolate (60–70% cocoa solids), grated

*12 ovenproof espresso cups*

SERVES 4

Preheat the oven to 150°C (300°F) Gas 2.

Put the milk, cream and sugar in a medium pan and scald by bringing to just below boiling point. Remove the pan from the heat.

Whisk together the egg yolks with the whole eggs in a large bowl, then whisk in the scalded milk. Stir in the vanilla extract. Strain the mixture through a fine sieve and divide into 3 equal parts.

Flavour one-third of the custard with the white chocolate, one-third with the milk chocolate and one-third with the dark chocolate, and stir each until the chocolate has dissolved. Divide each flavoured custard between 4 of the espresso cups. Stand the cups in a roasting tin half-filled with hot water. Cover each cup with a small sheet of aluminium foil, or spread a large sheet over the whole roasting tin, tucking it in at the edges.

Bake for 20 minutes. The desserts are cooked with they are set around the edges but still slightly wobbly in the middle. If they're still not quite cooked, you may need up to 35–40 minutes, depending on your cups. Remove the foil, being careful not to let any condensed water drop onto the custards. Lift out of the roasting tin and leave to cool. Refrigerate overnight and bring to cool room temperature before serving.

*For all those who love mint and dark chocolate, this is for you, especially if you're a fan of after-dinner mints covered in dark chocolate. The mousse is deceptively simple to make and is a good dinner-party standby. My niece adores this dessert – another winner for older children.*

# MINT CHOCOLATE MOUSSE

150 g dark chocolate (60–70% cocoa solids)

4–6 dark chocolate-covered mint fondants (preferably After Eights), chopped

4 eggs, separated

2 tablespoons golden caster sugar

4 tablespoons double cream

1 teaspoon powdered gelatine

2 tablespoons chopped chocolate mint sticks, or frosted mint leaves and 250 ml double cream, to decorate

*4 little pots or glasses*

SERVES 4

Melt the chocolate with the mint fondants according to the instructions on page 17. Leave to cool slightly. Using an electric whisk, whisk together the egg yolks and sugar in a large bowl until thick and mousse-like, then whisk in the melted chocolate and the cream.

Sprinkle the gelatine over 4 tablespoons water in a small, heatproof bowl and leave to soak and swell for 2–3 minutes. Put the bowl into a pan of simmering water and stir until the gelatine has dissolved. Whisk into the chocolate mixture.

Working quickly, whisk the egg whites in a clean, dry bowl until stiff but not dry, then fold into the chocolate mixture with a metal spoon.

Divide the mousse between the pots. Scatter with the chopped mint sticks, then refrigerate until set. Alternatively, whip the 250 ml cream and use to decorate the mousses, along with the frosted mint leaves. Leave at cool room temperature for about 20 minutes before serving.

*This is a great dessert to make when you've got some cranberries stashed in the freezer or during the Christmas season when they are fresh. Their fruity sharpness beautifully complements the chocolate. The result is a tempting, deep red compote hidden under a layer of darkest chocolate mousse. This is for adults only!*

# DRACULA'S DELIGHT

### CRANBERRY COMPOTE

150 g fresh or frozen cranberries

75 g golden caster sugar

2 tablespoons Cointreau

### CHOCOLATE MOUSSE

200 g best-quality dark chocolate (60–70% cocoa solids)

3 tablespoons strong espresso

25 g unsalted butter, cubed

1½ tablespoons chocolate liqueur

3 large eggs, separated

*four deep glasses or pots*

SERVES 4

To make the cranberry compote, put the cranberries in a small pan with a splash of water and the sugar. Bring to the boil and simmer for 5 minutes until all the cranberries have burst and the compote is thick. Stir in the Cointreau, then spoon into the glasses. Leave to cool.

To make the chocolate mousse, melt the chocolate with the espresso and butter according to the instructions on page 17. Stir in the liqueur. Stir in the egg yolks while the chocolate mixture is still hot – this will cook them slightly.

Using an electric whisk, whisk the egg whites in a clean, dry bowl until they form firm peaks. Using a metal spoon, stir a large spoonful of egg whites into the chocolate mixture to loosen it, then gently and evenly fold in the rest. Spoon the mousse on top of the cranberry compote. Cover and refrigerate for at least 6 hours or overnight.

*This is chocolate divinity! Very rich and very smooth – use your favourite dark chocolate and you won't be disappointed. Make this for a special occasion, as it looks very elegant and can be made well ahead of time (although there is a lot of washing up to do). You can use white or dark chocolate for dipping the sponge fingers. Once this is set, I sometimes spoon a little chocolate liqueur over the sponge fingers before turning it out. You can even sprinkle the surface of the marquise with chocolate shavings. This makes a good birthday cake.*

# CHOCOLATE MARQUISE

250 g dark chocolate (60–70% cocoa solids), plus 100 g for dipping

about 18 sponge fingers (boudoir biscuits)

100 g unsalted butter, softened

100 g golden caster sugar

2 tablespoons unsweetened cocoa

1 teaspoon good-quality instant coffee granules, ground to a powder

3 egg yolks

2 tablespoons chocolate liqueur, rum or brandy

300 ml double or whipping cream

pouring cream, to serve (optional)

*a 500-ml charlotte mould, soufflé dish or 500-g loaf tin, lined with non-stick baking parchment*

SERVES 8

Melt the 250 g chocolate and the 100 g chocolate separately according to the instructions on page 17. Leave to cool slightly until warm but not cold.

Dip the ends of the sponge fingers into the 100 g melted chocolate, tap off the excess and lay on a tray lined with non-stick baking parchment to set.

Line the sides of the prepared mould with the dipped fingers, making sure they go in dipped tips first. You may have to shave down the last finger to give a tight fit.

Now have three mixing bowls at the ready. In one bowl, cream the butter with half the sugar until very white and fluffy. Beat in the cocoa and coffee powder.

In the second bowl, whisk the egg yolks with the liqueur and the remaining sugar until really pale and doubled in volume.

In the third bowl, whisk the cream until it forms soft peaks.

Beat the 250 g melted chocolate into the butter mixture. Take a spoonful of the egg yolk mixture and beat it into the chocolate mix to loosen it, then fold in the remaining egg mixture. Finally, carefully fold in the cream. Pour the mixture into the mould. Tap gently to settle the mixture and refrigerate for at least 4 hours. Trim off any protruding sponge fingers, then turn out onto a plate to serve. It is rich enough on its own – but you could also serve it with pouring cream if you like.

*There's something very special and exotic about the subtle marriage of chocolate and cardamom. Grinding the caster sugar, cocoa and cardamom seeds together to a powder makes a perfumed and sophisticated coating for the surface. Grinding your own will give more flavour, but you can mix ready-ground cardamom with icing sugar and cocoa for a similar effect. This is really one gigantic truffle, so it is best served cut into very thin slices.*

# CHOCOLATE CARDAMOM TRUFFLE CAKE

### AMARETTI BASE

150 g amaretti or ratafia biscuits

60 g unsalted butter

60 g golden caster sugar

### CARDAMOM TRUFFLE FILLING

600 ml double cream

4–6 green cardamom pods, lightly bruised to open them

750 g dark chocolate (60–70% cocoa solids), grated

55 g unsalted butter, cubed

4 tablespoons chocolate liqueur

### CARDAMOM COCOA SUGAR

3 cardamom pods

50 g caster sugar

50 g unsweetened cocoa

*a 25.5-cm cake tin with a removable base, base and sides lined with non-stick baking parchment*

SERVES 10–12

To make the amaretti base, finely crush the amaretti in a food processor or put them in a plastic bag and crush with a rolling pin. Melt the butter and sugar in a pan over gentle heat, then stir in the biscuit crumbs. Press the mixture evenly over the base of the prepared cake tin and refrigerate for 20 minutes.

To make the cardamom truffle filling, put the cream and cardamom pods in a pan and heat until almost boiling. Remove from the heat and leave to infuse for 20 minutes.

Meanwhile, put the chocolate and butter in a saucepan. Strain the infused cream through a sieve onto the chocolate (the cream will be warm enough to melt the chocolate). If it doesn't melt, warm over very low heat, stirring occasionally, but do not allow it to boil. Stir in the liqueur, then leave until almost cold, but not set. With an electric whisk, whisk the chocolate mixture for a couple of minutes – this will give a lovely airy texture. Pour onto the amaretti base. Leave to cool, then cover and refrigerate for at least 6 hours, or up to 48 hours before serving.

To make the cardamom cocoa sugar, remove the black seeds from the papery cardamom pods and put the seeds in a spice grinder with the sugar and cocoa. Grind to a powder. Carefully remove the cake from the tin and peel off the lining paper. Set on a chilled serving plate and sift the cardamom cocoa sugar evenly over the top. Serve immediately, cut into very thin slices.

*This is another dessert that would make a wonderfully indulgent birthday cake adorned with golden candles. Children would probably prefer it made with really good-quality milk chocolate or you could stir white chocolate chips into the plain chocolate batter. It may seem against all chocolate rules to melt chocolate and water together (see page 17), but it works if they go in at the same time – the water keeps the chocolate fluid.*

# MARBLED CHOCOLATE CHEESECAKE

### CHOCOLATE CRUMB BASE

175 g chocolate-coated digestives, chocolate chip cookies or chocolate Bourbon biscuits

75 g unsalted butter

25 g soft light brown sugar

### MARBLED CHOCOLATE FILLING

150 g dark chocolate (60–70% cocoa solids), chopped

750 g full-fat cream cheese, at room temperature

250 g golden caster sugar

1 vanilla pod, split lengthways, seeds scraped out and set aside, or 1 teaspoon vanilla extract

2 large eggs

150 ml whipping cream and 100 g white chocolate, grated and chilled, to decorate (optional)

*a springform cake tin or deep sandwich tin with a removable base, 23 cm diameter, lined with non-stick baking parchment*

SERVES 10

Preheat the oven to 180°C (350°F) Gas 4. Carefully grease the sides of the cake tin and refrigerate until required.

To make the chocolate crumb base, crush the biscuits in a food processor or put them in a plastic bag and crush finely with a rolling pin.

Melt the butter and sugar in a small pan over gentle heat, then stir in the biscuit crumbs. Press the mixture evenly over the base of the prepared cake tin. Bake for 15 minutes, then remove from the oven, lightly press the biscuit base down again and leave to cool completely. Reduce the oven temperature to 160°C (325°F) Gas 3.

To make the marbled chocolate filling, melt the dark chocolate and 50 ml water according to the instructions on page 17, then keep it warm.

Put the cream cheese, sugar and vanilla seeds, if using, in a large bowl. Using a wooden spoon or electric whisk, beat until soft and creamy. Put the eggs and vanilla extract, if using, in a separate bowl and whisk well. Gradually beat the eggs into the cheese mixture. Pour approximately 250 ml of the mixture into a jug, then pour the remaining mixture into the cake tin.

Stir the warm chocolate into the reserved cheese mixture. Pour the chocolate mixture in a wide zigzag pattern over the surface of the cheesecake, edge to edge. Draw the handle of a thick wooden spoon through the pattern, zig-zagging in the opposite direction so the mixtures give a marbled effect. Do not overwork or the pattern will be lost. Keep it simple and the edges neat.

Bake for 20–25 minutes, or until the cheesecake starts to puff slightly around the edges but is still very soft in the centre. Carefully transfer the tin to a wire rack and loosen the edges of the cheesecake with a thin-bladed knife. Leave to cool slowly by putting a large upturned bowl over the cheesecake. When completely cold, refrigerate for at least 3 hours before removing from the tin.

When you are ready to serve the cheesecake, remove it from the tin. For a special flourish, whip the cream and spread the sides lightly with a very thin layer. Press the grated white chocolate into the cream. Cut generous slices with a hot knife.

# TRUFFLES
## AND SWEETS

# ITALIAN CHOCOLATE TRUFFLES

*Look at the picture opposite and you will understand why a chocolate truffle is called a truffle – because it looks very like its dark and earthy savoury sibling, the black truffle, and is just as precious to chocoholics. This is a classic truffle recipe – very rich and dense, and reliant on the best-quality chocolate that you can afford. For real truffle addicts, stir a little truffle honey or a drop of real truffle oil into the mixture – the flavour combination is quite mysterious but delicious – but keep them away from other chocolates as the flavour can wander!*

150 g dark chocolate (60–70% cocoa solids)

100 g salted butter, cubed

1 egg yolk

2 tablespoons Mozart Black Chocolate Liqueur or dark Crème de Cacao

1 teaspoon truffle honey or a drop of real truffle oil (optional)

unsweetened cocoa, to dust

*a baking sheet, lined with non-stick baking parchment*

MAKES ABOUT 15 TRUFFLES

Melt the chocolate according to the instructions on page 17. Beat in the butter, then the egg yolk, liqueur and truffle honey, if using. Cover with clingfilm and refrigerate for about 1 hour, or until set.

Sift some cocoa onto a plate. Using a teaspoon, scoop the chilled chocolate mixture into rough mounds, shape into a knobbly truffle shape in your hands, then drop into the cocoa. Roll it around until it is completely covered and put on the prepared baking sheet. Layer in an airtight container between sheets of greaseproof paper and refrigerate for up to 5 days or freeze for up to 1 month.

# WHITE CHOCOLATE COCONUT TRUFFLES

*These are delicious morsels of white chocolate married with coconut which has been infused with coconut liqueur. For these truffles, I like to use Crazy Jack's Organic desiccated coconut or sweetened, tenderized coconut because they are both softer and nicer to eat than ordinary, drier desiccated coconut. The truffles look best rolled in a shaggy coat of shredded coconut, but use more desiccated if you can't find it.*

100 g desiccated coconut (see above)

1 tablespoon clear Crème de Cacao (optional)

2–3 tablespoons coconut liqueur or white rum

½ teaspoon vanilla extract

55 g unsalted butter

3 tablespoons double cream

225 g white chocolate (over 25% cocoa butter), chopped

1 egg yolk, at room temperature

100 g shredded coconut, to coat

*a baking sheet, lined with non-stick baking parchment*

MAKES ABOUT 20 TRUFFLES

Put the desiccated coconut in a bowl and pour over the liqueurs and vanilla extract. Mix well, cover and leave until the liquids have been absorbed.

Put the butter and double cream in a large, heatproof bowl over a pan of barely simmering water. The bowl should not touch the water. When melted, remove the pan from the heat and add the chocolate to the bowl. Stir until melted and smooth. Lift the bowl off the pan and stir in the egg yolk and the liqueur-infused desiccated coconut. Beat well, then leave to cool. When cold, cover with clingfilm and refrigerate for about 2 hours until firm.

Spread the shredded coconut on a plate. Scoop up the white chocolate mixture and roll into 2.5-cm balls. Roll each truffle around in the shredded coconut to coat, then put on the prepared baking sheet, cover and refrigerate for 1 hour. Layer in an airtight container between sheets of greaseproof paper and refrigerate for up to 5 days or freeze for up to 1 month.

*I like to pass round a mound of these surprisingly warm and mysterious truffles instead of dessert. You could use chilli-infused vodka instead of the liqueur or brandy. Make your own chilli vodka by infusing a couple of whole fresh red chillies, pierced here and there with a needle, in 300 ml vodka. Seal, leave in a cool, dark place for 2 weeks, then strain. The candied chilli threads used to decorate these truffles are always a talking point. Remember that they can be very hot!*

# CHOCOLATE CHILLI TRUFFLES

CHOCOLATE CHILLI TRUFFLES

275 g dark chocolate (60–70% cocoa solids)

50 g unsalted butter, cubed

300 ml double cream

1¾ teaspoons pasilla chilli powder (see page 143)

2 tablespoons chocolate liqueur, brandy or Armagnac

2 tablespoons unsweetened cocoa mixed with ½ teaspoon pasilla chilli powder (see page 143) and 1 tablespoon icing sugar, to dust

CANDIED CHILLI THREADS

250 g sugar

3 large, red chillies, deseeded and shredded

*a baking sheet, lined with non-stick baking parchment*

MAKES ABOUT 20 TRUFFLES

To make the chocolate chilli truffles, melt the chocolate with the butter, cream and chilli powder according to the instructions on page 17. The mixture should be just tepid. Stir only occasionally (over-mixing will make it grainy). Stir in the liqueur. Leave to cool until the mixture has thickened slightly, then whisk for 2–3 minutes with an electric whisk. Refrigerate until firm.

Scoop out teaspoonfuls of the mixture and roll into balls. Put the truffles on the prepared baking sheet and refrigerate. Sift the cocoa-chilli-sugar mixture onto a plate. Carefully roll each truffle in the powder, then set on a tray lined with non-stick baking parchment. Refrigerate until firm. Layer in an airtight container between sheets of greaseproof paper and refrigerate for up to 2 weeks or freeze for up to 1 month. Leave to stand at room temperature for 5 minutes before serving. Serve scattered with candied chilli threads.

To make the candied chilli threads, put the sugar and 300 ml water in a medium pan. Bring to the boil for 1 minute. Add the chillies to the sugar syrup, reduce the heat and simmer for 25 minutes. Remove the pan from the heat and leave to soak in the syrup for 24 hours, if possible. Lift the chilli threads out of the syrup with a fork, drain well and arrange on non-stick baking parchment. Store in layers in an airtight container for up to 1 month.

# COLETTES

*I have tried in vain to find out the origin of the name of these pretty little truffles. All I know is that the French writer Colette was very fond of chocolate and real black truffles, so maybe these were named after her. I like to paint the cases with a layer of dark chocolate then a layer of white chocolate. They are fun to make and certainly have the wow-factor of a handmade chocolate. Use your favourite truffle mixture for the centre if you prefer, or the recipe for Chocolate Ganache (page 136).*

200 dark chocolate (60–70% cocoa solids)
100 g white chocolate
150 ml double cream
2 tablespoons chocolate liqueur, kirsch, brandy or rum
20 amarena cherries, drained (optional)

*a paintbrush*
*20 paper petits fours cases or a chocolate mould with 20 indentations*
*a piping bag fitted with a star nozzle*

MAKES 20 COLETTES

Melt 100 g of the dark chocolate and all the white chocolate, separately, according to the instructions on page 17. Using a paintbrush, paint the inside of the paper cases or chocolate moulds thinly with the dark chocolate and refrigerate until set. Paint a coat of white chocolate on top of the dark and refrigerate until set.

Put the cream in a small pan and bring to just boiling point, then remove from the heat and add the remaining dark chocolate. Leave the chocolate to melt, then stir until smooth. Leave to cool, then stir in the liqueur. Leave to cool at room temperature for at least half an hour, or until thick enough to pipe. You can refrigerate the mixture briefly if you are short of time.

Put a cherry, if using, in each case. Beat the chocolate cream well, then spoon into the piping bag and pipe on top of the cherries. Refrigerate until ready to serve.

Carefully peel off the paper cases or prise the chocolates out of their moulds to serve. Refrigerate in an airtight container for no more than 3 days.

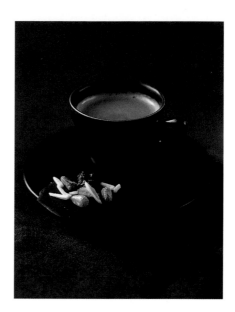

# CHOCOLATE COINS

*These little treats are known in France as mendiants. Each chocolatier has his or her own house speciality, so the sky's the limit when it comes to choosing the toppings. Make them as colourful as possible and don't forget to soak the dried fruits in lovely liqueur first.*

250 g dark chocolate
chilli powder and gold leaf, to decorate

SUGGESTED TOPPINGS
raisins, soaked in 1 tablespoon rum and 100 ml boiling water
crystallized ginger, chopped
flaked and toasted almonds
toasted hazelnuts and pistachios
salt crystals

MAKES ABOUT 20 COINS

Melt the chocolate according to the instructions on page 17. Remove from the heat and leave to cool for 3–4 minutes, or until very slightly thickened. Cover a large, heavy baking sheet with 2 layers of clingfilm. Spoon 20 small pools of chocolate onto the clingfilm. Leave to set for no more than 2 minutes, then scatter with toppings. Finish with a hint of chilli and a touch of gold leaf. When the coins are completely set, ease off the clingfilm. Serve with after-dinner drinks and coffee.

*These are little mouthfuls of chewy caramel studded with fruit and nuts and dipped in your favourite type of chocolate. Mix and match the fruit and nuts, but make sure that some of the nuts are finely chopped to bind it all together. Florentines are a little tricky to make at first – you need to adjust your cooking times to suit your oven – but this becomes easy after the first batch. Once you serve them, they disappear in no time!*

# CHOCOLATE-DIPPED MINI FLORENTINES

225 g mixed blanched almonds, hazelnuts and pistachios

50 g unsalted butter

175 g golden caster sugar

25 g plain flour

300 ml double cream

175 g dried apricots, chopped, or candied mixed peel

50 g dried sour cherries, dried cranberries or quartered glacé cherries

225 g dark chocolate (60–70% cocoa solids) or about 75 g each of white, milk and dark chocolate

*two 12-hole mini-muffin tins, greased and dusted with flour*

MAKES ABOUT 100 MINI FLORENTINES

Preheat the oven to 190°C (375°F) Gas 5.

Chop half the nuts roughly and the remainder quite finely. Set aside.

Put the butter and sugar in a heavy-based pan and heat gently, stirring, until the sugar has almost dissolved (it will not dissolve completely). Add the flour and continue to stir over gentle heat until the mixture is smooth and comes away cleanly from the sides of the pan. Do not let the mixture catch or go brown. Remove the pan from the heat and slowly beat in the cream until smooth. Stir in the nuts, apricots and cherries.

Drop half-teaspoonfuls of the mixture into the prepared mini-muffin tins. Be mean with your measurements here – the florentines will spread. (You will need to bake the mixture in several batches.) Bake for 8–9 minutes, or until the florentines have spread and are bubbling and lightly browned at the edges. Remove from the oven. At this point the florentines will still be very soft. Leave to cool for a couple of minutes, then flip out of the tins with a small palette knife and leave to cool on a wire rack. Repeat with the remaining mixture.

Melt the chocolate according to the instructions on page 17. (If using different types of chocolate, melt them separately.) Dip the florentines halfway into the melted chocolate. Set them on a tray lined with non-stick baking parchment. Leave to set, then store them layered between non-stick baking parchment in an airtight container. Serve with after-dinner coffee and liqueurs.

*This is a rich and decadent fudge for those with the sweetest of teeth to serve as a pick-me-up with mid-morning coffee or after dinner with a chocolate liqueur. Nibble a chunk and let it melt on your tongue – heaven! If you don't have a sugar thermometer, boil the sugar mixture for 5–7 minutes to the 'soft ball stage' – that is when a drop of mixture dropped into very cold water forms a soft ball that collapses when it is fished out of the water.*

# CHOCOLATE MAPLE FUDGE

500 g golden granulated sugar

100 ml maple syrup

150 ml milk or double cream

150 g unsalted butter, cubed

150 g dark chocolate (60–70% cocoa solids), broken into pieces

2 teaspoons vanilla extract

salt crystals

*a sugar thermometer (for best results)*

*a shallow 18-cm square (or similar-sized rectangular) baking tin, lightly greased*

MAKES ABOUT 800 G

Have a large bowl of cold water ready in the sink.

Put the sugar, maple syrup, milk, butter and chocolate in a large, heavy-based pan and stir over gentle heat, without boiling, until the sugar has dissolved.

Bring the mixture to the boil and boil hard until you reach 116°C (240°F) on a sugar thermometer, stirring every now and then to prevent it catching. As soon as you reach this temperature, remove the pan from the heat and dip the base in the bowl of cold water to stop the mixture cooking. Add the vanilla extract and beat well with a wooden spoon until the fudge becomes thick and creamy, with a grainy texture. Pour into the prepared baking tin, smooth the surface and leave to cool for 5 minutes. Press some salt crystals all over the fudge.

When it is almost set, score squares in the surface of the fudge with the tip of a sharp knife. When completely cold, turn out and cut into squares.

**Variation:** For a nutty alternative, fold in 100 g chopped walnuts or pecans immediately after beating the fudge.

# CHOCOLATE ALMOND-STUFFED FIGS

*I like to dip these alternately in white and dark chocolate, but it just depends on your favourite types of chocolate and your mood.*

20 large, ready-to-eat dried figs
100 g good-quality marzipan
1 tablespoon chocolate liqueur
20 whole almonds or walnut halves
250–300 g dark chocolate (60–70% cocoa solids)

*a large baking sheet, lined with non-stick baking parchment*

*20 paper cases*

MAKES 20 STUFFED FIGS

Slit the figs open down one side with a sharp knife. Knead the marzipan and liqueur together and divide into 20 even pieces. Wrap each nut with a piece of marzipan and use to stuff the cavities of the figs, squeezing them into shape – don't worry if the filling protrudes.

Melt the chocolate according to the instructions on page 17.

Push a fig onto the end of a skewer or dipping fork and dip into the melted chocolate until lightly covered. Set on the prepared baking sheet and refrigerate until set. Place in paper cases and store in an airtight container, layered between sheets of non-stick baking parchment, at cool room temperature.

# CHOCOLATE ARMAGNAC PRUNES

*There's something really luscious about biting into these chocolate-dipped sweetmeats – the chocolate coating snaps to reveal the soft, rich Armagnac-infused prune with its creamy nut centre. I don't recommend keeping these in the fridge, as they tend to go 'sweaty'.*

20 Agen prunes (or other large juicy variety), stoned
100 ml Armagnac, heated
100 ml boiling water
20 whole almonds or walnut halves
250–300 g dark chocolate (60–70% cocoa solids), chopped

*a large baking sheet, lined with non-stick baking parchment*

*20 paper cases*

MAKES 20 CHOCOLATE ARMAGNAC PRUNES

Slit the prunes open down one side with a sharp knife. Put in a medium bowl with the Armagnac and boiling water, and toss to coat them with the liquid. Put a saucer on top of the prunes to push them under the alcohol, then leave to soak for 2 hours.

Drain the prunes and pat dry on kitchen paper. Stuff the cavities with an almond or walnut and squeeze to enclose.

Melt the chocolate according to the instructions on page 17.

Push a prune onto the end of a skewer or dipping fork and dip into the melted chocolate until lightly covered. Set on the prepared baking sheet and refrigerate until set. Place in paper cases and store in an airtight container, layered between sheets of non-stick baking parchment, at cool room temperature.

# DRINKS, SAUCES
## AND GLAZES

*This is an instant mood lifter – make this drink when you are feeling a bit dejected and you cannot fail to feel fabulous. Watch out – it is quite potent! If you are feeling utterly miserable, the only answer is to top it with whipped cream and sink into comfort oblivion.*

# HOT SPICED RUM CHOCOLATE

600 ml milk

75 g dark chocolate (60–70% cocoa solids), chopped

2 whole star anise

finely grated zest of ½ unwaxed orange

1 tablespoon orange-blossom or acacia honey

75 ml spiced rum

50 ml Grand Marnier or other orange liqueur

cinnamon sticks, to garnish (optional)

*a large glass, warmed*

*a silver or stainless steel spoon*

SERVES 2

Put the milk, chocolate, star anise, orange zest and honey in a pan and heat gently, stirring, until the chocolate has melted.

Remove and discard the star anise. Add the rum and Grand Marnier and liquidize in a blender or with a hand-held blender until completely smooth and frothy. Pour into a warmed glass with a silver or stainless steel spoon sitting in it to absorb the heat and prevent the glass from cracking. Garnish with cinnamon sticks, if using. Drink immediately and feel fabulous!

This drink can also be served chilled in the summer. Use 450 ml milk and heat as before but leave to cool (keeping the star anise in to infuse the milk). Remove the star anise, stir in the liqueurs and pour into a blender filled with a handful of ice cubes. Blend until smooth, then pour into a chilled glass, sip and feel restored.

*Churros are long, golden, finger-like Spanish doughnuts, deep-fried and rolled in caster sugar whilst still hot. They are eaten for breakfast, dipped into fantastically thick hot chocolate. They are also known as* chi-chis *in Southwest France.*

# SPANISH HOT CHOCOLATE WITH CHURROS

### CHURROS (MAKES ABOUT 12)

400 g plain flour

300 ml milk

2 large eggs, beaten

vegetable oil, for deep-frying

caster sugar or icing sugar, to dust

### SPANISH HOT CHOCOLATE

400 ml milk

¼ teaspoon allspice

115 g dark chocolate (60–70% cocoa solids), grated

2 egg yolks

*a piping bag fitted with a large, fluted nozzle*

*a deep-fat fryer (optional)*

SERVES 2

To make the *churros*, sift the flour onto a sheet of greaseproof paper. Put the milk and 300 ml water in a medium pan and bring to the boil. Shoot in the flour and beat vigorously with a wooden spoon, stirring until the mixture just begins to pull away from the sides of the pan (just like choux pastry). Remove the pan from the heat and leave to cool a little.

Add the eggs and beat until the paste is completely smooth and not too runny (you may not need all of the egg).

Spoon the mixture into a piping bag. Heat the oil in a deep-fat fryer or wok until a piece of dough sizzles as soon as it hits the oil. Pipe fingers of the mixture into the hot oil, snipping off 10-cm lengths with kitchen scissors. Fry the *churros* in batches of 4–6 until golden brown, then remove with a slotted spoon and drain on kitchen paper. Put some caster sugar or icing sugar on a plate and roll the *churros* in it to coat. Eat immediately, dipping them into the hot chocolate. Any leftover *churros* can be frozen and reheated in the oven.

To make the Spanish hot chocolate, put the milk and allspice in a small pan and bring to the boil. Add the chocolate and stir until melted, then whisk in the egg yolks. Stir over gentle heat until slightly thickened. Now whisk with a hand-held blender or a cappuccino frother, until frothy. Pour into cups and drink whilst hot. (Some say this is better made the day before and reheated.)

# CHEEKY MONKEY CHOCSHAKE

*This is a truly wicked, thick, alcoholic milkshake guaranteed to cheer up the chocoholic. I like to drizzle in extra warm chocolate sauce just before drinking it – stir with a long spoon and drink through a straw. If you didn't feel like a cheeky monkey before, you will after drinking this!*

Bitter Chocolate Sauce (page 135), warmed

1 medium, ripe banana

30 ml Crème de Bananes (see page 143)

50 ml clear Crème de Cacao (see page 143)

2 scoops vanilla or chocolate ice cream

2 tablespoons chocolate syrup or chocolate sauce

a good handful of crushed ice

*a tall glass*

SERVES 1

Peel the banana and break it into pieces.

Blend the banana, liqueurs, ice cream, chocolate syrup and crushed ice in a high-speed blender. Serve in a tall glass drizzled with warm Bitter Chocolate Sauce.

# CHEEKY MONKEY CHOCSHAKE (NON-ALCOHOLIC)

*This is one for the kids, or if you are off alcohol.*

1 medium, ripe banana

2–3 tablespoons banana milkshake powder

100 ml milk, banana milk or banana yoghurt drink

2 tablespoons chocolate syrup, chocolate sauce or chocolate-nut spread

2 scoops vanilla or chocolate ice cream

a good handful of crushed ice

a chocolate flake, to serve

*a tall glass*

SERVES 1

Peel the banana and break it into pieces.

Blend the banana, milkshake powder, milk, chocolate syrup, ice cream and crushed ice in a high-speed blender. Serve in a tall glass with a chocolate flake.

# CHOCOTINI

*A must for all chocoholics – I doubt 007 would approve, but it's definitely one for a Bond girl!*

unsweetened cocoa, to dip
2 parts vodka
1 part dark Crème de Cacao or other chocolate liqueur

*a martini glass, chilled*
*a cocktail shaker*

SERVES 1

Put some cocoa on a plate, wet the rim of the martini glass and dip it in the cocoa.

Fill the cocktail shaker with ice and pour over the vodka. Put on the top and shake really well for 1 minute. Remove the top and strain into the glass. Now slowly pour the Crème de Cacao into the glass, being careful not to touch the rim. The chocolate liqueur will sink to the bottom making a two-tone layered cocktail. Serve immediately and sip slowly.

# LE CHOCOLATIER

*A cool chocolate hit for a hot summer night. Float some more chocolate liqueur on top if you are feeling really devilish.*

1 part Mozart Black Chocolate Liqueur or dark Crème de Cacao
1 part white rum
150 g good-quality dark chocolate ice cream
1 tablespoon grated dark chocolate

*a tall glass, chilled*

SERVES 1

Put the chocolate liqueur, white rum and ice cream in a blender. Process at low speed until evenly blended and pourable. Pour into the chilled glass and sprinkle with the grated chocolate. Serve immediately.

# THREE WARM CHOCOLATE SAUCES

## WHITE CHOCOLATE SAUCE

*This is one for all those who love white chocolate – it is very rich and sweet, so a little will go a long way.*

250 ml single or double cream
100 ml milk
250 g white chocolate (over 25% cocoa butter), chopped

MAKES ABOUT 600 ML

Put the cream and milk in a small pan and bring to just below boiling point. Remove from the heat and leave to cool for 2–3 minutes. Add the white chocolate and stir until completely melted. Serve warm.

If reheating, do so over gentle heat. Do not allow to boil or the sauce can thicken and seize.

## BITTER CHOCOLATE SAUCE

*The flavour of this sauce will rely on the type of chocolate you use, so choose it carefully. You may like to add a little sugar to sweeten it.*

225 g dark chocolate (60–70% cocoa solids), grated
200 ml double or whipping cream
40 g unsalted butter, cubed

MAKES ABOUT 450 ML

Put the chocolate and cream in a small pan. Heat very gently, stirring occasionally, until melted and very smooth. Do not allow to boil. Whisk in the butter and serve warm.

## RICH CHOCOLATE FUDGE SAUCE

*The only way to make a true fudge sauce is to include soft brown sugar. This gives it that fudgy taste and texture. I use cocoa here, as the sauce is boiled and chocolate would be too delicate to handle the heat.*

175 ml double cream
150 g soft light brown sugar
50 g golden caster sugar
75 g unsweetened cocoa, sifted
50 g unsalted butter, cubed
1 teaspoon vanilla extract
a pinch of salt

MAKES ABOUT 450 ML

Put the cream, brown sugar, caster sugar and cocoa in a medium pan. Gradually bring to the boil, stirring occasionally. Turn down the heat and simmer gently for 1 minute, stirring to help the sugars dissolve. Stir in the butter, vanilla extract and salt. Serve warm.

# CHOCOLATE GANACHE

*This is a very versatile 'icing' – it can be used to cover and fill cakes, make light truffles and be piped into shapes. Needless to say it is very rich, and needs to be beaten to thicken and aerate it. Use according to the specific recipe.*

450 ml double cream
250 g dark chocolate (60–70% cocoa solids), grated

MAKES ABOUT 750 ML (ENOUGH TO FILL AND COVER A 23-CM CAKE)

Put the cream in a heavy-based pan and bring to just boiling point. Add the chocolate and stir, then leave to stand for about 15 minutes, or until the chocolate has completely melted. Stir until smooth, then cover the surface with clingfilm to prevent a skin forming. Leave to cool completely, then refrigerate.

When you are ready to serve, bring to room temperature again, beat it lightly to soften (do not over-beat) and use according to the specific recipe.

# GLOSSY CHOCOLATE GLAZE

*A very useful glaze for dipping small cakes and biscuits into, as it will stay soft and shiny. When using to cover a cake, leave the glaze to cool until it is starting to thicken and becomes spreadable, then use about one-third of the glaze to smooth over the cake and act as a primer for the final coat. Once you have spread over a rough base coat that fills in all the nooks and crannies, gently warm the glaze back to the ideal temperature (see below) and pour the whole lot directly onto the centre of the cake. Spread it to the edges of the cake with a metal spatula and leave it to trickle over the sides naturally – you should have a streak-free cake. A cake turntable is useful here.*

250 g dark chocolate (60–70% cocoa solids), grated
175 g unsalted butter, cubed
1 tablespoon golden syrup

MAKES ABOUT 400 ML (ENOUGH TO GLAZE A 25-CM CAKE)

Melt the chocolate with the butter and golden syrup according to the instructions on page 17. If using to glaze a cake at room temperature, make sure the glaze is at the ideal temperature of 32–33°C (90–92°F). If using on a chilled cake, the glaze should be at 31–32°C (88–90°F).

# CHOCOLATE CREME PATISSIERE

*Here's a wonderful thick custard to use as a filling for all sorts of cakes and pastries. Make a plain version by omitting the cocoa and using a total of 35 g flour, cornflour or potato starch.*

600 ml milk
2 egg yolks
75 g golden caster sugar
3 tablespoons unsweetened cocoa
2 tablespoons plain flour, cornflour or potato starch
½ teaspoon vanilla extract

MAKES ABOUT 700 ML

Put the milk in a small pan and heat until just about to boil. Remove the pan from the heat. In a heatproof bowl, whisk the egg yolks with the sugar, then whisk in the cocoa and flour. Whisk in the hot milk. Return to the pan and heat gently, stirring until starting to thicken. Once it reaches a very slow boil, simmer for 2 minutes, then stir in the vanilla extract. Use immediately or pour into a bowl, cover the surface with clingfilm, leave to cool, then refrigerate for up to 1 week.

# CREME ANGLAISE

*This is a classic thin egg custard that can be served warm or cold with most desserts instead of cream. It can be left plain, infused with spices like cinnamon or cardamom, or flavoured with a favourite liqueur.*

1 vanilla pod, split lengthways
300 ml milk
1 tablespoon golden caster sugar
2 egg yolks
2 tablespoons brandy, Armagnac or bourbon (optional)

SERVES 4–6

Put the vanilla pod, milk and sugar in a small pan and heat gently. Bring almost to the boil, then set aside to infuse for 15 minutes. Remove the vanilla pod. (Rinse and dry the vanilla pod and store in a sugar jar to make vanilla sugar.)

Put the egg yolks in a bowl, beat well, then pour in the infused milk. Mix well and return to the pan. Stir with a wooden spoon over gentle heat until the custard coats the back of the spoon. Pour into a cold bowl and stir in the brandy, if using. Cover the surface with clingfilm, leave to cool, then refrigerate until needed.

**Variations:**

**Chocolate Crème Anglaise:** Stir in 30–50 g grated dark chocolate once the custard has thickened. Once melted, stir in some chocolate liqueur instead of brandy.

**Coffee Bean Sauce:** Infuse 1 tablespoon finely ground espresso coffee powder with the vanilla pod, milk and sugar.

# CHOCOLATE BUTTERCREAM

*This makes the smoothest, most heart-stopping buttercream ever, for filling or covering cakes and biscuits. Be sure to leave plenty in the bowl for licking! It will keep for up to a week in the fridge and can be frozen for up to 6 months. Bring to room temperature before re-beating or it will curdle.*

6 egg yolks

200 g golden caster sugar

500 g unsalted butter, softened

200 g dark chocolate (60–70% cocoa solids), melted (see page 17) and cooled

3 tablespoons chocolate liqueur (optional)

*a sugar thermometer (optional)*

MAKES ABOUT 750 G (ENOUGH TO FILL AND COVER A 23-CM CAKE)

Using an electric whisk, beat the egg yolks until pale and creamy.

Put the sugar and 150 ml water in a small pan and heat gently, stirring occasionally, until the sugar has dissolved. Bring to the boil and boil hard until it reaches 116°C (240°F), or the 'soft ball stage' on a sugar thermometer (see page 121). Immediately remove from the heat and pour the hot syrup onto the egg yolks in a thin steady stream, whisking continuously until the mixture is a pale, thick mousse. Cream the butter in a separate bowl then beat in the melted chocolate. Beat this into the egg yolk mixture, then beat in the liqueur, if using. Use at room temperature, when it will be easiest to spread.

**Variations:**

**White Chocolate Buttercream:** Substitute the same amount of white chocolate for the dark chocolate and use a little vanilla or orange liqueur instead of chocolate liqueur.

**Raspberry Buttercream:** Take 350 g frozen raspberries and thaw them in a sieve placed over a bowl. Press them gently with the back of a spoon to squeeze out the juice. Put the juice in a small pan and boil it hard until it has reduced to 3 tablespoons.

Press the raspberries through the sieve and mix the strained purée with the reduced raspberry syrup and a teaspoon of freshly squeezed lemon juice. Sweeten with sifted icing sugar to taste. Beat this into the buttercream instead of the chocolate or even WITH the white chocolate. Use a little natural pink food colouring if the colour isn't as bright as you would like.

# GLOBAL CHOCOLATE AND THE FUTURE

For 3,000 years, chocolate had been a bitter drink venerated by the elite. By the mid-twentieth century, due to the advances in chocolate-refining technology, chocolate could be manufactured on a vast scale to be eaten, not drunk. Drinking chocolate all but disappeared, leaving cocoa – a drink available to all – and the ubiquitous chocolate bar. This new commodity spread throughout the world and was pioneered by familiar names such as Fry and Cadbury in the UK, Menier and Poulain in France, Lindt and Suchard in Switzerland and later, Hershey in the USA. Today, consumers are asking for more than ever – they want high-quality, organic, Fairtrade chocolate and they're willing to pay for it.

There is a revolution happening throughout the food world. We have begun to ask questions about what we are eating, where it has come from and how it was produced. We are beginning to ask for quality and starting to recognize it – and the same is happening with chocolate.

In the past, in an attempt to manufacture a uniform product suitable for the mass market, cheaper and inferior beans were used, often unfermented, then over-roasted and conched for a long time to give a neutral but consistent flavour and smooth texture. Now, in the twenty-first century, we crave more than sweet, bland, creamy chocolate bars. We are rediscovering the true meaning of good chocolate through a burgeoning selection of independent factories using antique techniques and artisan chocolatiers employing state-of-the-art equipment. In their hands, the art of true chocolate-making is being kept alive and ever refined. We are in an age that is ceaselessly in search of the new, the different, the indulgent, the covetable. The consumer is becoming more demanding, chocolate-making is big business and the industry has become very competitive. Larger manufacturers are realizing that they have to compete with these smaller, luxury producers to stay ahead of the game, so they have begun to produce their own specialist chocolate bars alongside their everyday products.

## IT'S ALL IN THE GENES

"The spirit of chocolate is bringing us back to the true path." So says Murray Langham, author and chocolate creator. Who would have thought that chocolate has become so important to world economy that in the UK we have The International

Cocoa Germplasm Database (ICGD). It sounds rather sci-fi, but it is an information service based at the University of Reading. The project aims to collate information on the origins, characteristics and availability of cacao germplasm and to make this available to researchers. This conjures up images of rows of test tubes and labs full of glowing light, but in reality the germplasm bank is really a huge botanic garden. Research is done into cacao genes to trace the origins of the first wild plants and use their natural survival tools to improve susceptibility to pests and diseases in modern plants (which can decimate an entire harvest).

The second part of the ICGD is The International Cocoa Quarantine Centre, which operates to ensure that this international exchange of germplasm can be satisfied without transferring pests and diseases from one cacao-growing region to another. There are currently 350 clones available for exchange and a further 100 undergoing quarantine. The University of Reading took over responsibility for cacao quarantine from the Royal Botanic Gardens at Kew in 1985 and receives funding from all over the world, supplying material for international clone and hybrid trials. The current quarantine procedure involves a two-year visual observation period to check for latent viral infections, and research is under way to accelerate the quarantine process. This research enables growers to experiment with improved varieties. In fact, due to some very clever research into Criollo, some growers, encouraged by enlightened chocolate companies, have been able to graft pure Criollo onto hardy Trinitario rootstock. This will mean that the king of cacao – the rare and coveted Criollo – will be able to be grown in quantity once more so real chocolate fanatics will be able to taste and experience chocolate aromas that haven't existed in the last 100 years. Domori, an Italian chocolate manufacturer, started replanting true Criollos in 1997 using seeds from the geneplasma bank in Trinidad. CIRAD (a French agricultural research centre) is helping to revive the native Nacional cacao plant in Ecuador and the Criollo in Madagascar. Chocolate bars boasting a content of a certain variety of bean will in future have to be genetically certified. This is all quite incredible, really – who would think that this amount of research is going into the humble chocolate bar?

So the future looks to be set in single-derivation chocolate bars made from 'heirloom' beans, treated with respect at every stage of manufacture. Small production methods coupled with careful attention to harvesting, fermenting, roasting, blending and grinding all combine to make good chocolate. Even the humble Forastero handled in the right way can make good chocolate, as the Swiss-owned Callebaut company has shown. Specialist or gourmet chocolate accounts for only 2% of the total world trade, and although it will never rival the sales in the mass market, there is and will be a blossoming choice out there, enough to suit every mood and palate.

## FAIRTRADE CHOCOLATE

Today, good chocolate is fashionable, but at a price. It is expensive, but small-time growers certainly don't reap the rewards and some of them have actually never tasted a chocolate bar.

This is where the Fairtrade mark comes in. The Fairtrade mark is an independent consumer label that aims to guarantee a better deal for disadvantaged producers in the developing world. Fairtrade standards are set by the international certification body FLO (Fairtrade Labelling Organizations International).

It is worth remembering that not all Fairtrade products are organic and not all organic products are Fairtrade. The two certification systems are independent of each other.

## ORGANIC CHOCOLATE

Even where products are not certified Fairtrade, many organic chocolate manufacturers do make a deliberate point of buying their cacao ethically (which is a good selling point for them), and many of them publicize this information on their products or websites. For example, Montezuma's have a 'Trading Fairly' policy that includes ensuring that ingredients come from sources where growers get a fair price. Indeed buying organic

chocolate is better for the environment from many points of view, and also may be better for health. Cacao is one of the most heavily sprayed crops in the world. Pesticides in developing countries can include chemicals such as lindane, which is linked to serious health problems including blood disorders and breast cancer. Organic cacao trees are grown with minimum use of pesticides – only four pesticides are permitted under organic production. This organic production should be encouraged in the tropical cacao-growing regions as it will sustain and preserve the surrounding biodiversity.

Organic chocolate often contains more cocoa solids than non-organic chocolate, and is not permitted to add any nasty hydrogenated fat, known to be harmful to health and widely used in mass-produced brands. The emulsifier lecithin is a permitted non-organic ingredient. Organic milk chocolate is made using organic milk products where high standards of animal welfare are adopted, including the infrequent use of antibiotics. Organic milk is higher in levels of some beneficial nutrients, particularly short-chain omega-3 essential fatty acids, as well as vitamin E and the antioxidant beta-carotene. Organic agriculture preserves the quality of the soil itself, so that foods produced often taste better and contain more nutrients. Organic products must be certified by a recognized certification body, for example The Soil Association. These bodies are regulated under EU law, and 'organic' is defined in EU law. There are many organic certification bodies throughout the world. When a UK-certified chocolate manufacturer uses cacao beans from another country, the UK certifier will contact the overseas certifier, and will obtain inspection reports and details of inputs and outputs, to ensure that the overseas standards conform to EU standards. This process is called establishing 'equivalence' and is rigorously applied. Suppliers of organic cacao beans are carefully certified and checked.

If the future is to be bright for chocolate and chocolate-growers we must learn the difference between good-quality and bad-quality chocolates, create a demand for high cocoa solids, be curious about bean varieties and how they are treated after harvest and what the factory methods are. Better chocolates aren't overpowered by additional and unnecessary flavours. Good, true chocolate speaks for itself as it slowly melts on the tongue releasing all the aromas so carefully captured on its journey from bean to bar.

# WEBSITES AND MAIL ORDER

## GENERAL INFORMATION ABOUT THE COCOA TRADE

www.worldcocoafoundation.org

www.icco.org
The International Cocoa Organization

## MISCELLANEOUS CHOCOLATE INFORMATION

www.mexicolore.co.uk
*Wonderful site dedicated to teaching all things Aztec and Mexican. Costume and prop hire. Demonstrations and workshops. Delightful.*

www.chocolatetherapy.com
*New Zealand-based website with online chocolate shop. Change your chocolate – change your life! Visit for very interesting chocolate philosophy, psychology and blog.*

## CHOCOLATE ONLINE

www.seventypercent.com
*THE site for the chocolate lover – chocolate shop, forum, blog, info and events – make this your homepage!*

www.chocolatetradingco.com
*Chocolate Trading Company is the largest online chocolate shop in the UK, specializing in fine chocolates from around the world, from cocoa to couverture. Chocolate club, shop, magazine, info and much, much more.*

www.chocolate.co.uk
The Chocolate Society
Tel: 0845 230 8899
*Including delightful Valrhona chocolates.*

www.plaisirduchocolat.com
Plaisir du Chocolat Salon de Thé
251–253 Canongate
Edinburgh EH8 8 BQ
Tel: 0131 556 9524
*Fab online shop of Edinburgh-based artisan chocolatier and salon de thé, serving pâtisseries,*

decadent chocolate desserts or a demi-tasse of Bertrand's celebrated Chocolate Espresso and more.

www.cocochocolate.co.uk
*Coco specializes in fine organic and ethically traded chocolate that is made with high cocoa content and real cocoa butter. Fabulous online shop (bars, nibs, cocoa butter) as well as Edinburgh chocolate house with informed staff. They even serve liqueurs and muscats that enhance the chocolate experience.*

www.hotelchocolat.co.uk
*Real, authentic and exclusive chocolates by post and through Hotel Chocolat stores. Also a Chocolate Tasting Club. They have their own historic cocoa plantation, the Rabot Estate, in the West Indies.*

www.artisanduchocolat.com
*Mail-order chocolate bars made from rare cacao beans – Criollo and Trinitario from single plantations in South America, the Caribbean and Asia. Plus porcelain chocolate pots (chocolatières), beautiful handmade chocolates and gifts.*

www.swisschocolatebox.com
*Online supplier of leading Swiss brands, based in the UK, but will ship overseas.*

www.barry-callebaut.com
*Barry Callebaut, headquartered in Switzerland, has been producing cocoa and chocolate products for more than 150 years. The world's leading manufacturer of high-quality cocoa and chocolate products from bean to shelf, with strong traditional roots in Europe.*

## CHILLIES AND CHILLI POWDER

www.coolchile.co.uk
*Comprehensive selection of whole and ground chillies including pasilla chilli powder.*

Also sell Mexican hot chocolate sets.

www.chileseeds.co.uk
*Grow your own chillies from seeds. All kinds of dried chillies, whole and ground, including pasilla chilli powder.*

www.seasonedpioneers.co.uk
*Crushed pasilla chillies.*

## GOLD AND SILVER LEAF

www.ediblegoldleaf.co.uk
*Includes powder, flakes and leaf.*

www.surbitonart.co.uk
*Edible gold and silver leaf sheets and flakes; edible gold and silver paints and sprays.*

www.squires-shop.com
*Edible gold leaf flakes.*

## FLAVOURINGS AND LIQUEURS

**G. Costa and Co Ltd**
Aylesford
Kent ME20 7NA
Tel: 01622 717 777
*Importers of Star Kay White's Pure Chocolate Extract, a fat-free chocolate flavouring made by an alcoholic extraction of a blend of natural cacao beans.*

www.thedrinkshop.com
*Every liqueur imaginable online – arrives beautifully packaged. White Mozart Chocolate Liqueur, Black Mozart Chocolate Liqueur, chocolate-infused vodkas, chocolate schnapps, Chocolate Cream Liqueur, Creme de Cacao (dark and clear), chocolate mint liqueurs, chocolate orange liqueurs.*

## CHOCOLATE-MAKING EQUIPMENT

www.homechocolatefactory.com
Tel: 020 8939 9000
*Incredible Surrey-based online store that has EVERYTHING for the home chocolate-maker, including bulk chocolate blocks,*

callets/pistoles, thermometers, moulds, tempering machines, foil wrappings, boxes.

www.gourmetsleuth.com
*California-based company which exports outside the USA. All sorts of chocolate goodies, from black stone metates, wooden molinillos, chocolate, chillies and chilli powders to Mayan/Mexican drinking chocolate sets.*

www.chocolatealchemy.com
Informative and passionate chocolate site. Fairtrade cacao beans from Dominican Republic, Ecuador, Ghana, Madagascar, Panama, Papua New Guinea and Venezuela, plus cacao nibs, chocolate-making equipment and tools and much, much more. Will ship outside the USA.

## CHOCOLATE COURSES AND TASTINGS

**Melt**
www.meltchocolates.com
59 Ledbury Road
Notting Hill
London W11 2AA
Tel: 020 7727 5030
*Chocolate heaven! Beautiful shop, handmade chocolates and truffles, kitchen visits, tastings, bespoke service.*

**Paul A. Young**
www.payoung.net
33 Camden Passage
Islington
London
N1 8EA
Tel: 020 7424 5750
*Presentation kitchen, cookery and chocolate workshops and chocolate shop.*

# INDEX